MW00477658

EXTENDED FAMILY

EXTENDED FAMILY

ESSAYS ON BEING IRISH AMERICAN FROM
NEW HIBERNIA REVIEW

EDITED BY

JAMES SILAS ROGERS

To Shawn, one of the true pioneers of Irish-American Studies

DUFOUR EDITIONS

[signature]

11 APRIL
2013

First published in the United States of America, 2013
by Dufour Editions Inc., Chester Springs, Pennsylvania 19425

© James Silas Rogers, 2013

All rights reserved. No part of this publication may be reproduced or transmitted in any form or by any means, electronic or mechanical, including photography, recording, or any information storage or retrieval system, without permission in writing from the publisher.

Copyrights for the contributions in the work are held by their respective authors.

ISBN 978-0-8023-1355-3

Cover Image: Carrick-a-Rede rope bridge
Courtesy of the Northern Ireland Tourist Board ©2012

Library of Congress Cataloging-in-Publication Data

Extended family : essays on being Irish American from New Hibernia review / edited by James Silas Rogers.
    pages cm
  ISBN-13: 978-0-8023-1355-3 (paperback)
  ISBN-10: 0-8023-1355-8 (paperback)
  1. Irish Americans--Ethnic identity. 2. Irish Americans--Biography. 3. Extended families--United States. 4. Extended families--Ireland. 5. Ireland--Relations--United States. 6. United States--Relations--Ireland. I. Rogers, James (James Silas) II. New Hibernia review.
  E184.I6E93 2012
  306.85'7--dc23
                                                            2012044549

Printed and bound in the United States of America

For Larry O'Shaughnessy
with admiration and gratitude

ACKNOWLEDGMENTS

New Hibernia Review is copyrighted by the University of St. Thomas. The journal has been the flagship program of the university's Center for Irish Studies since 1997. The university has generously permitted use of the material that originally appeared in *New Hibernia Review*.

Here are the original publication dates of the various works included in this volume, listed by the author's name and in the order of oldest to newest:

Eamonn Wall, volume 2, number 4 (Winter, 1998), 9-23
James E. Doan, volume 3, number 3 (Autumn, 1999), 9-19
Lawrence J. McCaffrey, volume 4, number 3 (Autumn, 2000), 119-127
Aífe Murray, volume 6, number 1 (Spring, 2002), 9-17
Daniel Tobin, volume 6, number 4 (Winter, 2002), 44-54
James Liddy, volume 7, number 1 (Spring, 2003), 9-13
Thomas B. O'Grady, volume 8, number 2 (Summer, 2004), 9-23
James Murphy, volume 8, number 3 (Autumn, 2004), 12-17
Maureen O'Connor, volume 10, number 1 (Spring, 2006), 9-16
Brigittine M. French, volume 11, number 1 (Spring, 2007), 9-24
Christine Cusick, volume 11, number 4 (Winter, 2007), 9-16
Charles Fanning, volume 13, number 1 (Spring, 2009), 9-19
Brian Nerney, volume 13, number 3 (Autumn, 2009), 9-20
Elizabeth Creely, volume 15, number 4 (Winter, 2011), 9-15

You can find more information about the *New Hibernia Review* at:
www.stthomas.edu/irishstudies/hibernia

CONTENTS

Broadenings

Misgivings

~

INTRODUCTION

Extended Family comprises one long poem, ten personal essays, and three articles that were written with primarily an academic audience in mind. All of these works originally appeared in the quarterly journal of Irish Studies, *New Hibernia Review.* Since 1996, when the first copy of the journal was presented to Michael D. Higgins–then the Irish minister for arts and culture, and now the president of Ireland–*New Hibernia Review* has made a point of opening each issue with a memoir or personal essay in addition to the fully annotated articles that form the core of its content.

This collection came into existence when at a certain point, I realized that *New Hibernia Review* had accumulated a striking body of work, grounded in the lived experience of Irish and American writers, that drew close to the question, What does it mean to be an Irish American?

I've called this anthology *Extended Family*, recognizing that the word "extended" works on several levels. We probably first think of an extended family as the constellation of kinship that radiates out from the individual–which it certainly does mean. Or we might think of "extended" as meaning the ties of ancestry and affection that obtain in both countries. And "extended" can mean stressed, the way a debtor is over-extended.

But the most apposite use of the word is not the most familiar. It's borrowed from developmental psychology, where the scientist Ulric Niessnet has offered the term "the extended self" to describe that point in child development when a child begins to realize that he or she "exists outside the present moment." That is precisely the point of departure for the writers here. As a group, all seek to locate their experience in a story, in a place, and in a time other than their immediate world—a common and a humanizing impulse. Such "extension" is one of the under-recognized benefits of an ethnic identity in our times, and at its best, offers an antidote to the placelessness and obsession with the present that marks modern life.

One of the critical buzzwords that is buzzing most loudly these days is "hybridity," the not-so-provocative assertion that immigrants and their descendants negotiate with and reassemble identities from both countries. That claim appears beyond argument. Much more interesting, it seems to me, are the places where the hybridity does not "take." Irish Americans, like other hybrids, are pushed or pulled by inherited—and often unexamined—ideas regarding who they are and where they came from. Throughout *Extended Family*, we encounter Irish Americans whose relationship to the land of their ancestors is marked by vagueness, a divided heart, and sometimes by outright bafflement. The authors of these essays are certain that being Irish in America conveys something distinctive—even if they are not always clear what that distinctiveness is, nor necessarily pleased when they find out.

Few Irish Americans today would think of themselves as exiles, in the way that Kerby Miller's celebrated *Emigrants and Exiles* described the notion as a perception of being driven out of their homeland. Yet, although the political implications of the exile model were given up long ago, at another level it still affects the consciousness of millions who call themselves Irish. The exile mentality suggests that although there was a rupture in the Irish national family – "her exiled children in America" in the words of the 1916 Easter Proclamation – there was also a profound continuity between the Irish at home and the Irish abroad. The residue of that idea no doubt provides part of the reason that so many accounts of Irish travel, including James Murphy's opening essay here, employ the trope of coming home.

Still and all, none of the essays collected here is that simple.

The act of putting together an anthology always provides themes and patterns that had not been noticed before. That was certainly the case with this book. Even though I had read and edited all of these works as they went into the journal, I had completely failed to notice something big: that when the essayists here reflect on a parental relationship, in all but a few cases it is the relationship with his or her father.

We might read quite a bit into that fact. If the authors here are representative (as I think they are), then one of the unexpected conclusions to be drawn is that, notwithstanding the cult of motherhood in Irish and Irish-American life, the task of understanding what it means to be Irish frequently entails a reconsideration of one's father. Of course, recent Irish memoir abounds with bad fathers: Frank McCourt's drunken dad, Nuala O'Faolain's philandering father, the authoritarian policeman who rules in John McGahern's *Memoir*. Such toxic parents are nowhere to be found in these pages. The worst we can say of the fathers in *Extended Family* is that they could be puzzling, or that they may not have been as communicative as their children might have liked.

That quality of enigma is a metonym for Ireland. It might well be that one's relationship with the father must function in the realm of myth and imagined connection. Our authors may be perplexed by their fathers; more often than not, they are perplexed by the meaning of Irishness, too.

Which makes their fascination with Ireland all the stronger. In an essay called "Imagination's Home," the Australian poet Vincent Buckley introduced a wonderfully useful concept for understanding the diasporic imagination when he posited the idea of Ireland as a "source country"– that is, Ireland "is a source in the sense that the psyche grows from and in it, and remains profoundly attuned to it" even if, like Buckley, one was raised thousands of miles away. As we read these accounts, we regularly find the writers describing a profound feeling of connectedness to the landscape of Ireland, or across generations, even as they describe Ireland as a place of unresolved family trauma or buried pain.

Crucially, Buckley's approach places the experience in the psyche. The truth is that the Ireland of our imagination is a vastly more interesting place than the Ireland of the real world could ever hope to be. The essays and memoirs in *Extended Family* look into that interior world from a range of viewpoints. The linking thread is that one way or another, each of the authors starts from the proposition that the full story has not been told. Or, to refine that further, that a story has been told–by parents, or society, or by critical opinion–but it has been told in ways that do not satisfy the authors here.

Inescapable, in these accounts, is the reality of loss. Memoir may well be the genre best suited to register loss.

In all but a few of these Irish-American memoirs, an awareness of what's gone, of what's been kept away from the narrator, or of what never happened, runs just below the surface, as present as the drone of a bagpipe.

The haunted grounds of the New World and the Old inform "The Narrows," Daniel Tobin's long poem that opens this collection. (The Irish taste for anomaly is alive and well: it just seems right to open an essay collection with a poem.) Tobin's poem sets out many of the themes that percolate though the book. Loss is here, but so is the expansive sense of belonging to a great historical narrative. When at one point Tobin undertakes genealogical research (as do many of the writers who follow), the project raises more questions than it answers; speculation is the hand-maiden of family history. And "The Narrows" suggests something else that will grow clear in the later essays—that the Irish-American experience walks very near to sadness.

The prose essays that follow appear under four broad thematic headings, the first of which is "Recoveries." We begin with a homecoming. James Murphy recounts with deliberate simplicity the story of his father's one and only trip back to Ireland, to family and fields in Leitrim he had left forty years earlier. Opening with the bald fact that there are no photographs of his parents' childhood, "Find-ing Home: Aughkiltubred, 1969" is at bottom a story of restoration. Though the father worried that he would not be able to pick up the threads snapped four decades ear-lier, he easily found himself at home in Ireland. The unforeseen dimension was that the son also connected to Ireland, in ways that would shape him for the rest of his life; as in any memoir, the real subject is the narrator's own consciousness. Buckley's idea of the source country is vivid in James Murphy's story.

Christine Cusick's "Tourmakeady Snow" shares much with the opening essay. It too involves a newly widowed parent, her father. And it too involves a felt gap with the personal past. Her father's father had left Ireland in the 1920s, and rarely spoke of his life there; for that matter, he rarely spoke at all. Cusick thus foregrounds one of the pervasive themes of this book, the fact of silence. The truth is that the people whom Wilde said were "the greatest talkers since the Greeks" show at least an equal gift for saying nothing. Moreover, life on the other side of the Atlantic seems, if anything, to have potentiated a talent for keeping their mouths closed. Every author in this book must engage with silence, denial, willed forgetting—all variations on the familiar non-strategy for dealing with trauma, *We're not going to talk about it.* There is nothing uniquely Irish about family secrets, of course; but there may be something distinctly Irish about the intensity of the silence that surrounds them. And yet, in the parish register of a small Mayo town, Cusick and her father find information that puts an end to decades of speculation.

Brian Nerney's "Stories from Down Cellar" overturns an enforced silence. Working backward from a short, once-off conversation with his father, Nerney uncovers the specifics of a family tale concerning his grandmother, the daughter of immigrants, who had witnessed a murder and testified at the trial. In a sense, keeping that secret came to define the family experience: we get the feeling that Nerney needs to know the story in order to fully understand the family experience, but also that he has somehow violated a trust by telling the truth. Memoir is, fundamentally a quest to retrieve memory; but it is also a dialogue between past and present. If worldviews did not change over time, memoir would be mere information. Nerney's inclination to reveal the truth collides with the earlier generations' insistence on keeping secrets. From the beginning, he knows instinctively that Irishness was a key to understanding the full dimensions of the family's reticence. But what he understood Irishness to mean differed from his forbears' understanding; the obsession with respectability that dominated the generations before him no longer makes sense.

The evolving, adaptive nature of ethnic identity is the unifying theme of the essays in the next section of the book, grouped here under the heading "Redefinitions." These three essays strike a more academic tone than others in this volume, though each is rooted in personal experience.

The shifting definition of Irishness is the exact subject of anthropologist Brigittine M. French's study of a Midwestern town that trades on its Irish past. Beginning with a quaint anecdote of her grandmother's appearance in the St. Patrick's Day parade in O'Neill, Nebraska, French retrieves more than a century of community history. In the early years of the settlement, the then-majority Irish citizens fully embraced the "exile" motif. A century later, only a few of the town's citizens have Irish ancestry–but the first thing visitors see is a shamrock-covered billboard that proclaims it "the Irish Capital of Nebraska." And when pushed to explain their understanding of Irishness, community members proudly report that in their minds it means the triumph of assimilation and inclusivity. Is this a radical change, or is it continuity?

James E. Doan's essay reminds us that a fluid ethnic identity is nothing new. Starting with his own great-grandmother, Gladys Burke, who was of both Irish and Native American descent, Doan considers a fascinating aspect of colonial American history, the frequent marriages between Irish and Scots-Irish traders and the indigenous population. This, too, is another of many instances of the American "melting pot" that never was. Recent years have given us a spate of myth-makers who hold out the early Scots-Irish as a foundational element in a supposed American thirst for self-reliance. Another myth to bust; Doan finds that, at least for a time, the Irish-Indian mestizo population functioned well in both the Native and the colonizers' societies, and were at ease in both identities. This may be one of the great might-have-beens of the American story: the pluralism that the frontier fostered would have served the American people well in later generations, had it survived.

But as we all know, no such pluralism came to pass. Moving forward two centuries, Lawrence J. McCaffrey shows us that, until fairly recent times, much of the Irish urban population stayed ghettoized in the ethnic neighborhoods—chiefly owing to their unapologetic Catholicism. Hybridity was neither a reality nor an aspiration for these *isolatoes.* McCaffrey uses the redoubtable 1944 film *Going My Way* to explore this moment in midcentury America. Though easily dismissed as sentimental and superficial, McCaffrey argues that the film is a valuable cultural document. *Going My Way* enjoyed huge popularity among Americans of all backgrounds. Appearing in the context of the Second World War, Americans (white Americans, anyway) were already being encouraged to set aside their ethnic differences for the national purpose. The 1944 movie marks the point when the self-isolation of the Irish community—and the "otherness" imposed on them from without—began to crumble for good. For mainstream America, *Going My Way* offered the modest but necessary reassurance that the Irish were not so different after all.

The four essays that make up the next section, "Broad-enings," provide thoughtful appreciations of Irish arts and letters, and for each author a link to Irish creativity enters his or her own life story. The awareness that Ireland has produced an astounding number of fine writers is very much a marker of Irishness. No other group invokes its lit-erary tradition with the same élan. One would not expect to walk into a bar in the American South, for instance, and be greeted by a picture of Faulkner and Welty, whereas images of Yeats and Joyce are all but compulsory in an Irish joint. Admittedly, the decorations of an Irish pub may be a dubious window on Irish-American cultural val-ues. But popular culture does emerge from deeper sources; a felt connection to a literary tradition is more than orna-mental in Irish life.

For all of these writers, an Irish author (or in Charles Fanning's case, a work of art) functions something in the way that an icon might in a religious context—not as an object of veneration, but as a window between two worlds. The art and the artists on which these memoirists fix their imaginations fascinate them over long periods and connect them to a larger significance, a larger story. Often, the fas-cination comes tinged with mystery.

Thomas O'Grady was raised in Prince Edward Island and is now settled in New England. He traces his own life as a poet and a scholar to his bond to the seven-teenth–century Gaelic poet Dáibhí Ó Bruadair. O'Grady suspects, though he cannot prove, descent from the earlier poet (his mother's family name was Brothers, an Angli-cized variant of the Gaelic, and the family legends overlap in enticing ways). In the end, the bloodline hardly matters. What matters is that O'Grady apprehends his literary inheritance in a way that allows him to distill his Irish and his Maritime experiences into poetry. In this essay, he quotes at some length from his own work, moving us beyond the boundaries of the poem and into historical realities. We understand the poetry not as an extension of self or ego but rather, as the witness of a consciousness informed by the world outside the present moment.

Aífe Murray's essay ranges from nineteenth-century Ireland, to New England kitchens, to present-day San Francisco as she brings us into the braided story of Irish immigrants and one of America's canonical writers, Emily Dickinson. I have noted the centrality of fathers in these memoirs; Murray's essay stands apart by writing of, in effect, a literary mother and a literary midwife. Opening on a trip to South Tipperary, Murray goes on to dig into Dickinson's life in a place where previous biographers had not thought to look: in the immigrant milieu that surrounded the Belle of Amherst, and especially in the day-to-day assistance of her maid, Margaret Maher of Killusty, County Tipperary. But like any biographical study, the teller writes herself into the story, too. As Murray retrieves the interwoven lives of two nineteenth-century women—one of worldwide posthumous fame, and one who remained obscure in life and in death—she begins to hear whispers of her own life. In every setting, she heeds the poet Susan Howe's counsel to "trust the place to form the voice."

And what places the Irish wound up in! Brooklyn may be a familiar landmark in the landscape of Irish America, but Guatemala City is not – yet it was there, James Liddy reveals, that novelist Harry Sylvester wrote the thoroughly neglected novel *Moon Gaffney*. Witty, digressive, and hyper-opinionated, Liddy's essay also reveals his personal connection to the novel, in which the chief villain is modeled on his first cousin. Sylvester's novel might be subtitled

"When Irish Eyes Are Scalding"; it's a complete evisceration of the self-enclosed pieties of midcentury Catholic Brooklyn, a place where the descendants of recent immigrants were determinedly working to forget their former poverty and dependence. *Moon Gaffney*, and Liddy's playful riff on it, express the poles of the New World Irish cast of characters—"Croesus and Dorothy Day," as he records in the title of the essay.

In "Lodestone: Following the Emly Shrine," Charles Fanning recounts the enduring presence in his life of an eighth-century Irish art work, the Emly Shrine. For the last six decades, the medieval masterpiece has belonged to Boston's Museum of Fine Arts, an institution that played a large part in Fanning's childhood. The museum does not come off well, in this essay; Fanning documents the suspect story of how the shrine was acquired, and the saddening story of how the treasure has been willfully ignored since arriving in New England. It might come as a surprise for readers who know Fanning's extensive scholarship in Irish-American literature to find that his lifelong engagement with Irish-American writing was in some ways triggered by this small artwork, not much bigger than a cigarette pack. In the closing pages, he reflects on how the shrine could be thought of as a sort of metaphor for the subject of his own scholarly work, the buried literary traditions of Irish-American writing: eclipsed, ignored, and under our noses all along.

That reflective tone continues into the closing section, called simply "Misgivings." Daniel Tobin's opening poem asks, "Is this what it means to be an American?" It's a question Americans never cease to contemplate; part of what it means to be an American is the privilege of asking it. The last three essays speak in a meditative tone. In each, we meet an author giving voice to doubts, and at times, lamenting that the promise of America has been squandered or betrayed.

For Eamonn Wall, a family trip into the Black Hills sets him to wondering about the connection between identity and place. As a child in County Wexford, Wall knew in his bones that he was home, written into the place by virtue of his early experiences and the history he had inherited. But America exerted a pull, one that he now recognizes as traceable to the early influence of Westerns he saw as a boy at the Astor Cinema in Enniscorthy, County Wexford. Now a college professor in America, Wall remains fascinated both by the plurality of the United States and by the sheer variety of its landscape. Still, the trip to the Black Hills reminds him of the American history of brutality and exploitation. On the road, he intuits the spiritual presence that Native Americans found in those mountains. But he simultaneously warns against the blithe presumption that white Americans can claim such a sacred landscape as their own—no more than smug commentators can pigeonhole Irishness from afar. Wall's essay is an exercise in counterpoint; his reflections on what it means to belong to a place (or a tradition) are answered by reflections on what it means to be an outsider.

The landscape is a foundational presence in Elizabeth Creely's essay as well, an account that melds memoir and environmental writing. Like many of the authors in this book, Creely faced gaps in the record of her family. She had not scratched very deep before meeting a blank wall of forgetfulness. Nonetheless, she managed to piece together a sketchy lineage out of varied sources. Lacking a more substantive narrative, Creely turns to the place where all stories start, our life on the land. As best as she can tell, her family seems always to have lived somewhere near oak trees, both in Ireland and in her native California. When she reads a short news story that links a present-day threat to California's oaks to the same pathogen that brought the Famine, she registers an inherited sense of dread. She ends on a worried note regarding our wounded world.

Extended Family opened with a healing return; it closes with an uneasy one. Maureen O'Connor, the daughter of immigrants, spent all of her childhood summers in Ireland. Now she has settled there for good, and her parents have returned as well. But the family's return at the height of the economic boom brought with it an unsettling mixture of continuities and disruptions, especially for her father. The immigrant's return is a story that's been told many times, and it seems to always to come back to the question, Where is home? O'Connor's father finds that he is now defined by the act of leaving. One suspects that millions of others in the Irish diaspora might reach the same conclusion.

The restlessness registered by O'Connor's father might, in fact, speak to this collection as a whole. If anyone described in these pages could claim "hybridity," it would be him—but that condition offers little comfort. Perhaps the essays in *Extended Family* are asking us to reconsider whether the hybrid diagnosis suffices to describe the Irish-American experience. The thrust of Irish-American ethnicity is not a struggle to reconcile two incompletely integrated homelands. Nor is it a mere dilution or imitation of the real thing back in Ireland: with one or two exceptions, the essays in this volume make plain that the stressed element of Irish-American identity is always the American. But Ireland keeps coming back, like an underground river finding its way to the surface. To my mind, Buckley's notion of the "source country" provides the most accurate vocabulary for understanding the persistence of an Irish-American ethnic identity.

The authors we meet in this book have extended their Irishness in various ways. Some have set out to retrieve unique family histories; others have cast their nets wider, creating new interpretive frameworks through which to understand the group's historical experience. Some have located their lives in an Irish narrative by opening themselves to literature and art. Still others have simply paused to reflect, illuminating the widely shared experience of Irishness by approaching it with interiority. Most important, the authors here have extended their stories, and their insights, to us as readers. For that generosity of spirit, we can only be grateful.

James Silas Rogers
St. Paul, Minnesota

DANIEL TOBIN

❧

THE NARROWS
for Nora Ruane, ni Hughes

I. *Mural*

The way Lanning painted it, or Rivera–bright panels
on which the laborers huddle, shirtless, their flexed arms
bearing the full weight of the rail.
      Representative men,
without names but for Paddy, Dago, Gook,
so the foreman calls them, shotgun slung behind his back
as he rides towards the Iron Horse somewhere deep
in the continent:
      Death Valley and Donner Pass,
rock-faces sheer, indifferent–
       or patient, as if to say *This rabble won't last long.*

To the left: a native lounges on empty prairie, then
a wagon, homesteaders tying bales of hay,
a horse-drawn thresher.
      To the right: turbines
squat as bombs, stokers at a furnace, a mother and infant
climbing into a crowded cart that will disappear
down the cavern walls of this street. A woman
leans out a window in a posture of regret.

Someone leaving,
someone not coming back,
while dead center of the mural others hammer the ties:

lives scaled out of lives along the panorama's strict expanse. . . .

———————

My father drives the gaudy pink Rambler
down Bay Ridge Avenue to the Shore,
the great wooden pier jutting into the Narrows—flood-tide,
bright flow—where the ferry luffs against its moorings,
its wide iron ramp laid down for the line of cars that slow,
then roll snugly into its belly:
                    me in back between my mother
and her mother, Nora, who carries herself regally
as the Guggenheims whose children she nannied
when she first came over.

Quayside at Cobh,
under St. Colman's spire, she waited at the pier,
black Mayo dirt smoored into her shoes,
daughter of a remnant, of clachan and rundale,
cottier and meitheal, the big ships made imaginable
on postcards distributed at crossroads in the townlands,
on signs posted in market villages: Dominion,
Cunard, White Star Line—"Splendid Accommodation"
for the exile, for the *deorí*:

"There's nothing for you here."

———————

The tender putters to its floating palace,
in the distance, Spike Island, Davitt's Rock.
For days in steerage she's one of the thousand
packed inside, the bunks camp-hung and numbered,
the boat heaving
                    to the Atlantic, as though each roll
were prelude to an undertow.
It's nearly a week before she comes to the rail,
the ship steaming past Sandy Hook, the Moriches,
the Narrows a *causey*
                    "of a highway where sky comes down to water."
There the Statue stands, torch in hand
                    above the dumbstruck hordes,
above the gleaming cityscape, *caisleáin óir*,
castles of gold, mythic as Tír na nÓg.

                    She's alone
as she queues off the gangway for the Great Hall
with its iron bars, an assembly line
of stations and pens, its marble alive with tongues.

It is as if the *throughother* of her familiar fields
had changed in a dream she only now awakens to,
the manifest tag pinned to her lapel,
a gripped inspection card, barked commands
from the uniform at the gate, from the uniform on the stairs.
She stiffens as she's handled, so many hands, her eyelids
twisted back with a buttonhook, the man ahead marked
with chalk, a brusque X on his coat
                    before he's shuffled away.
What's your name? Where are you going? What's your trade?
Have you a job? Can you read this?

–"Let my sentence come forth from thy presence;
let thine eyes behold the things that are equal."–

Then the shower, a baptism, the old world washed free.

                    And she's through,
the Island behind her with its dormitories and detainees,
caged yard and infirmary, walls glyphic with names,
the ferry bearing her to open road–fifty years:
a husband, five children, a first son outlived. . . .

———————————

Her Brooklyn of ample hills rises behind us,
bricked-up, paved over
as our ferry pushes into the Narrows
for our trip west. Ahead: Todt Hill, the terminal
at St. George.
          Skyscrapers crowd to the brink of the Battery.

And as the boat loafs into the harbor–
                              a panorama of docks,
liners lumbering out to sea, tugs and tankers
where the bare steel towers of the bridge soar, half-risen,
over Gravesend,
          the Hudson pouring itself along the Palisades,
the Statue a green flame in the middle of it all.
                    And already
my grandmother is out of the car for a better view,
shoring her new hat against the wind.

II. *Archive*

How often have I dreamt this station's bare-bulbed dusk,
a distant clatter of wheels, the visible tremor
                              up the platform's spine
where pipe-water leaks along cracks of cement:
I look down the tunnel, watch the subway's double star
widen inside the passage, the din growing louder by the second,
my back braced against a pillar as the light
fans like a slow motion explosion along the ancient tiles
before the train bursts through, a cargo of bright rooms
riding the polished rails, filling the emptiness
of the ribbed archway:
                    The R Local at 86th and Fourth,
where I'd wait with my mother those few afternoons
we'd venture to the city.
                    Stay close, she'd tell me, don't go
by the tracks, watch for strangers. I'd keep near,
stop my ears against the screech.

———————

The rules are strict inside the archive—no food, no bags,
no talking beyond this point.
                    And don't forget
to take a number, line up for instruction
from the stern administrator, who, it turns out,
is politer than he looks, directing me patiently
in how to use the volumes of categories and codes,
as if these tomes were history's phone books,
as if each of us could dial our origins.

Registries, ships' lists, census reports, the boxes
        and their corresponding dates
piled ceiling high along the aisles
in the light's fluorescent haze.
        The archive is a Chinese box, a maze
that draws me further in, each filmed list
a laboratory slide of DNA—
                Nora Ruane, ni Hughes,
of Kilvendoney. Her stone in Calvary
reads 1900, though she lied about her age, recited
the rosary in her small kitchen afternoons
when I came home from school,
—"Get me a cruller, Danny, from Sally's,
and yourself a hamburger and I'll make some tea . . ."—

For as long as I knew her she lived apart
from my grandfather, Martin, immobile
in a nursing home, our visits
become flickers in an unlit room.
Though my mother kept his passport—
British Subject, 1918, aged twenty years—
in the hope chest with her keepsakes.

In a gray, dated box I find the likely reels.
                Whir of machines
in the viewing room, the tape unspooling its microscopic lists,
bright squares like the subway's lit-up windows
across the black bar of film.
                The cards, hastily typed,
run in spate down the screen where I sit, scanning the sounds
of names, until, finally, I read Martin Ruane,
arrived April 8th, 1920,
        S.S. Kaiserin Auguste Victoria.

But how did he travel from Ballyhaunis
to Liverpool, the Prince's Dock, where the Irish were thick,
as Hawthorne wrote, "like maggots in cheese?"

          And where did they meet, born
twenty miles apart, in different townlands?
      Not in the port, not in Claremorris.
For her name I need to scroll further back—-
               Harlan, Hellas, Hugo, Hughes:
ten Nora Hughes's—earliest 1910, most likely 1915—
arrived on *The Celtic* to New York out of Cobh.
Did they love each other?
           I heard of marriages arranged, families
gathered by county in their new neighborhoods.
In the photo she kept on her bedroom dresser
they looked so properly posed.

I remember how she grieved when he died,
keening her first son's name with her husband's
in the funeral parlor's smoky hall.

Let's say I can see them
          in the old apartment on Sixth.
In the dim light of that kitchen
Nora peels potatoes on newspaper;
Martin, a motorman, home from the subway,
turns on the radio while the baby
sleeps in his crib;
      at the table, three daughters,
a first son just back from play
who will die of meningitis within a week.

—"I'll never get over it," my mother tells me
years later, a seine of smoke
drifting through the room,
 lit by a whiskey glass.—

Or let's say it's long after the war, the whole family
moved to Pearl Court. The sisters play cards
as the stereo hums
                    The McNulty Family, The Clancy Brothers:
             Kitsch *clachan* in a beehive of brick.

Whiskey. Quarrels. Penny-ante.
Voices mingled in smoky fluorescence.
Nora in her housedress nursing
a shot and cigarette, dusk
fading through the slit blinds.

And let's say she predicts her own death, foreseen
in a dream, the way as a girl she saw
that man in his brown suit wandering
the fields of Kilvendoney
    who had died the day before. . . .

———————

All the way back on the train
                    I watch the faces
of those around me. What do I have
but this clumsy reel of memory, this world
whirring past that fumbles away,
though I long to scroll it back,
                    to thread the spool

into the jumbled record of who I am?
I bring my trace home,
                              even now
splicing the narrative together, sounding it out,
pasts made present already the past.

III. *West*

To begin, love: our fingers on the map's crimped horizon,
following roads that run inland from the sea,
tracing the way west
                    in the clear light of our rented room—
Lucan, Clonard, Horseleap, Athlone, the names
reeling off
                    lyrics sung to their own accompaniment,
all the way to Ballinrobe.
                              Outside, the teeming puzzle
of Dublin streets converges at the Liffey,
then out along the quays toward Kilmainham, Chapelizod.

                              It's all out of scale,
this naming and the thing named, as though the map
were territory,
                    and yet such frisson brings lift-off,
like the giddiness of our flight
above the Narrows, the city receding behind us, the bridge
grown small as a safety pin, clipping the islands
as we banked along the coast, leaving
the continent behind,
                    only a few boats below,
fish glistening into the ocean's huge nothing.

———————

Who cares if its all fiction, this romance of origins,
a farmhouse in a townland outside Ballinrobe,
stories rehearsed a hundred times
                              across a kitchen table?
How my grandmother had to leave, like her sisters
but one, Winnie, the youngest, turned back from Ellis Island,
a chalk "E" scratched on her coat, her eyes
already glazing under the buttonhook
                              into those two moons,
and her stooped
      as though searching for something lost.
            Or how Tommy, her brother,
ruled the house, and would not let her go
to visit family in America–
                  dollar bills pinned on walls
beside holy pictures, a brother and sister,
like an old couple, bent in silence before the hearth.

———————

Here, driving free of town, the rotaries
run clockwise, the roadway
a mirror image of our familiar path.

My grandfather might have traveled east
along a version of this route
to one of the channel boats moored along the Liffey.
"Scholar," his passport read.
                  Did he leave for the "better life,"
like the millions who left because they had to go?

From Brize to Ballyhaunis, all the way to Eden Quay,
he followed the path of the long meadow,

as though to join that earlier train,
those who starved in their sod hovels,
                        the sod itself
a last meal caking in their mouths.
And there was my grandfather, Martin, like Nora,
my grandmother, leaving by cart or train—who knows how?—

a generation later, finding their place
                        in the prospect
of a canvas too vast to envision whole.

———————

 Is that what it means to be an American,
discovering yourself in the distances?—
                Like a man on a Greyhound
that leaves the New York Port Authority
and takes the Lincoln Tunnel to the Interstate.
It's after dark, all the man can see are headlights
        passing, a blur of malls and sub-divisions.
He sleeps in his seat beside a stranger,
                        wakes when the bus pulls in
to a late night road stop. He's not hungry,
but feels in his gut a tremor
                        of loneliness
that grows as they pass through Ohio, Indiana,
the furnaces of Hammond and Gary
                fierce as Blake's Satanic mills
spewing into the boundless prairie sky.
He looks out for a thousand miles
at the hypnotic emptiness of wheat fields and cornfields,
        the cinematic grandeur of the Rockies,
and descends from the Wasatch

to the Great Salt Lake,
a sunset spreading over the earth
as on the Fifth Day. . . .
                What he wants
is to stand at the other end of it all, to see
the Pacific rolling into the headlands
like visible waves of light,
                  and then to turn back,
the bridge stretching out over the bay below him,
another Narrows,
       until he sees that there is no end,
just these waves of water waves of land
flung together,
        feeling on his face the rush of wind,
and inside him the growing thought that anywhere
might be home,
           since home has become nowhere.

———————

It is like our standing present now
before this ancestral house
          passed to unfamiliar hands,
its thatch removed years ago, a modern extension
jutting out back from whitewashed clay walls.
             No one home.
And as we peer through the window,
            the hearth inscribes its arc
halfway up the wall, its border painted brightly,
      an old-time kettle at the center.
Hearth, hearth, where the heart reminds itself–
         Winnie dead, Tommy dead,
a line of unknown faces trailing back,

fanning forward,
our own to be among them,
as if now were the space between facing mirrors
life's after-life of lives indwelling.

And already it's renewing itself,
the memory of our car ride across a country,
              that is not our own,
checking the map, stopping to find our bearings,
our lunch in a town called Gortaleam,
how we bickered about the right road,
but made our way—
              the church at the crossroads
in Robeen, the cemetery in the field
      where Winnie and Tommy are buried
with their parents, Sabena and Martin,
all the names on a single stone—
              then, so close,
losing our way again, stopping to ask directions
to Kilvendoney—its four farmhouses on stony ground
twenty miles from the Atlantic,
      how the old farmer leaned his windblown face
to our window before pointing us the way:

      —"Is it Hughes you're wanting?
      O, they're all gone."

Recoveries

JAMES MURPHY

༄

FINDING HOME:
AUGHKILTUBRED, 1969

September, 1930. Age sixteen, my mother, Kathleen Sloyan, the second of eight children, leaves her home in Ballyhaunis, County Mayo. She will marry, raise three children, and die in Brooklyn, New York, at age fifty-three, without ever returning home.

We have no photos of her as a child.

With my first wages as a paperboy, I bought her a 78-rpm record that had "Mayo" in the title. Her hug was a full world. Her eyes filled, and for years I bought her anything that had Mayo in the title. I still love the sound of the word Mayo.

March, 1924. Age twenty, my father, Patrick Joseph Murphy, the fifth of thirteen children, leaves his home in Cloone, County Leitrim. He will return forty-five years later, a year after the death of my mother, many years after the deaths of his own mother and father.

We have no photos of him as a child.

This is the story of his journey home. I went with him and met myself.

———————

In the Brooklyn world of my childhood, Ireland was always there on my mental horizon—in the rhythms of speech and turns of phrase of Irish people about the house; in the ballads about the old country and a moonlight in Mayo that could bring my mother to tears; in the Friday night card games in which a priest visiting from Ireland might occasionally loosen his collar and mutter a sort of curse when the Lord failed to fill his inside straight.

Ours was a world of aunts, uncles, cousins; the calendar had its comforting rhythm of gatherings for holidays, baptisms, communions, graduations. And the funerals. Always uncles, John, Michael, Frank, each death strange in its own way, each one driving my father deeper into himself.

I was eight when Uncle John fell over the banister on his way up to his apartment, dropped three stories, and broke his neck. I didn't really know him, but I can still see him falling.

Then, I was nine when Uncle Michael fell under the wheels of an IRT subway car. The family said it was the heart that gave way, dead before he hit the tracks, others whispered that he had jumped.

My Dad said his brothers had bad luck. Mikey must have had the old heart attack. John, another story, let him be, no point in going on about it, let it be, drop it.

Then, my godfather, Uncle Frank the bachelor, a large man with gruff manners whose hand swallowed mine when he shook it, his breath spoke of cigarettes, whiskey, and anger. I felt bonded to him as my godfather and a bit afraid of him at the same time.

He drank himself to death. I was thirteen when he died; my father was fifty and was burying his third brother in America. Years later, I would begin to understand his loss and the pain that he kept inside as the funerals kept coming. But then, I was young and my father's losses were distant. I went to my uncles' wakes and funerals and then came home, tired after a day of play with all the cousins.

I remember a deeper sense of loss about Uncle Frank's death than about John or Michael. Perhaps because I was older, the idea of death had begun to have meaning, but I also think that, despite my youth, I sensed Uncle Frank was a lonely and unhappy man, moving in a world too far removed from our Christmas dinners for me to understand.

He remains very much with me, since he is in my parents' wedding picture, the best man. The picture is on a table in our bedroom, so I see it at some level of my consciousness every day.

A lovely picture, taken in New York in a studio, light years way from Leitrim and Mayo. The whole picture speaks of Ireland, of emigration, and of change, especially the poses of the four men—my Dad, Uncle Frank, Mark Cummings, and John Foley, my Dad's best friend and himself off the boat like the rest of them. There they are in their rented tuxedos, probably for the first time in their lives, looking stiff, awkward, proud of themselves.

Emigrants to a new world, just starting out, so far from their homes. Why this formal studio photo session? I now realize that it was to send their word home that all was well, that they were prospering in the New World. The photo sent home says, "Not to worry, all's well."

In Aughakiltubred, parish of Cloone, County Leitrim, what could my grandparents, John Murphy and Bridget Maguire, possibly have thought when this picture arrived in the mail? There they are—two of their sons, Patrick and Francis, long gone from home and not likely to return; dressed in tuxedos for a marriage, one of their sons marrying a woman they would never meet, a formal occasion at which parents should be honored and basking in the glow of the moment, but there are no parents in these wedding photos. These parents are an ocean away from this wedding and will not be seen again by their children, and will know many of their grandchildren only in the stream of photographs that will try to shrink the distance.

I now know that such photos were regularly sent home to Ireland from the States—a steady chronicle of marriages and births. How many of these photos came in the mail over the years? And then, the stream of photos of grandchildren, an expanding family in America and Canada known to them only in these photos. Hard to imagine their sense of separation.

The distance between these two worlds of our family came to me one day when I came home from school and my Dad was there, home earlier from work than was normal. My intuition said that something wasn't quite right. News from Ireland—my grandmother had died. Naive, I don't think I had ever thought of my parents having parents. I really couldn't grasp the whole idea of it—my father had a mother, but she lived far away in this mysterious place we talked and sang about. I had a grandmother, she had died, my Dad would never see her again.

He sits there, silence fills the room, and I try to understand this mystery.

My Dad went home for the first and only time in 1969. My Mom had died the year before, and my sisters and I were especially aware that she had never managed a trip back home, so we gave the trip home as a Christmas present. Since he wouldn't risk such a journey on his own, I was more than willing to be his partner. A very exciting prospect for me, a chance to close the distance between the Ireland of my imagination and the reality.

But, while I was excited, I can't say that "Daddy," as we called him, was at first thrilled at the prospect. I think, in fact, that he may have been a bit intimidated by the whole idea. Since he hadn't been a letter writer, the links to Ireland had been maintained more by and between our aunts who passed the news on to us. After the deaths of his brothers, all his links to Ireland had closed down. Aunt Catherine called it a hopeless place. Aunt Rose had gone home once, come back, and said it was beyond hopeless. My Dad was a warm, loving man, full of sharp humor, always humming tunes he composed as he went along, but at the same time he was a man of few words, at least in terms of his personal feelings and experiences. I suspect that is, at least in part, an Irish trait, especially on the male side of the fence, but planning this trip energized him in a special way. He began to speak more about Ireland as the trip approached, he had lots of questions. He wanted to look good, so off we went to Sears and Roebuck on Bedford Avenue, our idea of high fashion. He was clearly nervous about the whole thing.

I don't think I fully understood his emotions at the time. Ours was to be a five-week trip, visiting Ireland and England. In each place, he had both his own and my mother's family to visit. Only as we talked on the plane did I realize that much of his nervousness came from worry that he might not like all these people. There he would be, for five long weeks, "at home," but in a world of strangers. So again, the distance that was so much a part of the lives of all the Murphys in America came to the fore, now a very real emotional reality. What would he have to say to his brother Eddie and to his sister Ellen? After all, they wouldn't be interested in baseball, one of his passions that was a sure indicator he had become a Yank. Would he like the world of in-laws he was about to meet for the first time?

As it turned out, there was no need to worry. Ireland fit him like a glove. He settled immediately into its rhythm, his brogue increasingly ever so slightly.

After a few days visiting with my mother's brothers and sisters in Mayo, it was off to Leitrim, the real goal of the whole trip. As we neared his home turf, he began to recognize landmarks, houses, churches. Now we didn't need the maps I had been studying so carefully since Shannon Airport. He became the guide.

We were closing distances.

"Turn here," "Make the next right," "If you turn here, you'll see Reynolds's place," and, "The next house should be John Lee's." Much had surely changed in forty years, but he knew this place; its houses and turns of the road had histories that he was remembering, this world of rough, marginal farmland, clearly not prosperous, was the place of their beginnings—all the Murphy boys and girls who wound up in Brooklyn, Manhattan, Canada, Rhode island, California, England, in jobs and worlds far removed from their parents who worked this stubborn Leitrim land to feed them.

When we came to the turn for Aughkiltubred, Daddy said we should keep going a bit further, make a few turns. He said there would be a place a bit up the road where we could buy some beer and stout to take up with us. Partly, he was testing his memory; partly, he was stalling.

His memory was good. There was indeed a place that was not really a pub in today's terms; rather, it was a sort of general store that also served as the post office and pub. Brady's, rough cement floor, and a few makeshift seats.

Only a few people in the place, and they watch us like hawks as soon as we come in. Daddy doesn't introduce himself, there is a deep quiet, we order two pints, tourists passing through.

I still feel his tension. He has gotten the place right in his memory; he has found it after all those years, but will this place know him? Then, some small talk about the weather: "Grand day," "Lovely," "Oh, it was bad this day a week."

We order twelve bottles to go, itself an insurance policy against disappointment.

And then a moment that closes all distances.

One of the men looks up and says, "Is it Packy Murphy?" There he is, Patrick Joseph Murphy, looking all too American in his Sears and Roebuck best, but he is surely close to home.

"Packy?"

No hesitation. "John Francis?"

Obviously, Daddy had recognized John Francis Mulvey or, at least suspected that he did. No dramatic hugs—a quiet handshake, and Mulvey, "We knew you were coming home. Eddie's expecting you above."

A remembered conversation, hopefully close.

Perhaps this moment is more in my own memory than in reality. Nonetheless, I remember it as a great release for Daddy. If he was OK with John Francis, surely he would be OK with his brother and sister. A few pints and some memory-lifted laughter helped to loosen his mood. Then, off up the hill to home.

When Uncle Eddie came out to greet us, I realized that this was surely an uncle. He and Daddy were so clearly brothers, their features so similar that they were as one, much more so than I remember any similarities between Uncle Frank and Daddy. Even before any words were said, their facial resemblance alone shocked me into memories of long dead uncles in America.

Great distances were closed in that meeting of two brothers who hadn't seen each other in forty years. Their greeting itself was not dramatic in any gesture or outward emotional demonstration. Brothers in more than looks, they deflected emotions, keeping their inner worlds to themselves. For all anyone could tell, they might have seen each other last week.

A handshake, no hugs. "You're welcome home . . . a fine day . . . Here, sit by the fire. . . ." Whiskey all around— the only public acknowledgment of a special occasion.

I count myself lucky to have been with my Dad when he finally went home. Little did I know on that special day, but in two years he would be dead. Eddie is now gone as well.

I like to remember the two of them, slowly and a bit awkwardly coming to know each other again. Aunt Maggie giving us a bit of tea, Daddy gradually settling into a rhythm of memory and laughter as old friends came by and nostalgia filled this small, warm, secure place. He was home, a circle had been closed.

He had lived his life far removed from this starting place, and now he was back—forty years after his starting out on the road to America. He had married and buried a wife, seen his three children grow up and do well in a world of baseball and rock n' roll; he had coaxed whatever he could out of a backyard Brooklyn garden, and he saw himself as quite the barbecue chef. He had labored on a bread van, tried his hand as a union organizer and, once, he had received a safe driver award that we all knew must have been a mistake.

That was his world as I thought I knew it.

But, as the days passed in Ireland, listening to him talk and remember with his friends, hearing the laughter about some forgotten wildness when they were all young bucks, watching him walk the fields with his brother, seeing the easy way he had with cattle, I realized that I had always known instinctively about this other world. Without my realizing it, Ireland had been one of my parents' gifts to me; perhaps without their even intending it as a gift, but here it was.

A whitewashed cottage in Leitrim, no running water, three rooms, a central fire—in this place, my Dad and the aunts and uncles of my growing up were all born.

All along on that trip, I had thought I was taking my Dad home. Now, I know he was showing me my own starting place. He took me home.

CHRISTINE CUSICK

~

TOURMAKEADY SNOW

Tourmakeady is a small rural district situated between Lough Mask and the Partry Mountains in County Mayo. It has a population of approximately one thousand people and remains, or perhaps struggles to be, a Gaeltacht area. My grandfather was born in this district in 1902 and lived there until he was twenty, when he left for West Hants Pool, England, and then for America. His name was Thomas Cusack, spelled with an "a" before he passed through the Ellis Island gates, spelled with an "i" once in America. I often wonder if this shift in spelling was his decision to claim a new start, or if it was his loss. He passed away seven years before I was born; and yet, even as a child, intrigued by the mysterious absence that I now understand as death, this man I would never know fascinated me.

It wasn't until I was an adult that I learned that—despite living with him for close to two decades—my father didn't know much more about his father than I did. He knew that my grandfather had left behind his father, Patrick Cusack, but my grandfather made only infrequent mention of a mother, and no mention of siblings. And there was, especially, no mention of why he decided, in the midst of his simultaneous hope for and disillusionment about an Irish Free State, to leave Ireland. When I would press my father for details with the thoughtlessness of a child, he grew silent until he could turn my attention to my grandmother, whom I had met and had the chance to know; she lived in our home during her last years of life. Once, at one of our Christmas teas that would last into the late hours of a cold evening, a second cousin claimed that my grandfather loved to laugh and joke, but my mother told me that she never heard such stories. In what has become the sad story of too many in the Irish-American working class, he labored long hours and drank too much. He drank even more after the death of his two daughters, the second of whom died in his arms.

On a warm August morning, in the car driving through the rough edges of Pittsburgh neighborhoods on the way to the Mt. Carmel cemetery to bury my own mother, my Uncle John told me that he and my grandfather had taken the trolley to this same cemetery nearly fifty years before, with a handmade wooden cross to put at the grave of his sister. They were poor, and this was to take the place of a more permanent stone. He told me this story with a surprising distance; listening to him recollect, as we rode together behind the hearse, it sounded as if he didn't know the characters within his own memory. My father was born just a year after his sisters died; unlike his three older brothers, my father would not know his family without the absent presence of these losses. The youngest of six, my father was born when my grandmother was forty-seven-years-old. She came to America from Derryherbert, County Mayo, just sixteen kilometers from Tourmakeady, although it would take separate journeys to America, and perhaps some recognition of home, to bring my grandparents together.

When I agreed to join my father, along with his brother John and his daughters, on a trip to Ireland my travel intentions were mostly related to work, with plans for archival research and literary conversations. I was in the midst of my dissertation project, an exploration of how a colonized people turn to the land in hopes of recovery and how the mnemonics of place might guide perspective, even while pulling one to the past. I was studying poetry, photography, and emigrant correspondence—and, with an academic eye, I pushed myself behind the glass of a critical lens, attempting to separate my work about loss and land from the rhythms of my own life, insisting too much that they are different realms.

My father and I had no fixed plan to visit my grandfather's home. Although we knew that Tourmakeady was not far from my grandmother's family, whom we intended to visit in Westport, when I mentioned making the drive there my father would only say, "We will see," covering his hesitation by heightened attention to the practicalities of travel. Knowing that he usually has good reason for few words, I did not press him.

While in flight over the Atlantic, I looked across to my father, whose fifty-five years did not match the deep contours of line that shaped his eyes and mouth. I wondered if he expected too much of this trip, if he hoped that that the new intonations of Irish voices, the new sights of gray skies cut by the greenness of the fields might replace, or at least lurk near, the empty spaces that come with grief. I placed my hand on his arm, trying to reach the loss of my mother, which even after more than a year's time was still moist beneath his skin, still numb beneath mine.

My mother's experience of cancer had given me occasion to think about this idea of finding, and losing, a home in a person, in the abstractions of their love, but also in the physical space they embody and the place they recall and signify.

My mother took her last breath in the still-dark hours of a summer morning, fourteen months after she was diagnosed with a brain tumor. I measure this experience with numbers, counting months, counting years, as if such quantitative detail holds meaning; but it does not. Cancer has a way of changing the form of time, of shifting perception, of annihilating even my mother's exquisite and tender life, cell by cell, moment by moment. And so my father and I shared an unspoken awareness that this trip was, in part, about letting go of the many deaths she suffered in her illness and of the haunting flashbacks that lingered and would catch me unaware in the minute's wait at a stoplight or in the cruel disguise of a dream.

In our own ways, we each longed for the overdue consolation of memory. I quietly worried that my father was incapable of receiving such comfort, a comfort that he spent much of his career selflessly providing to others. My father supported our family as a school social worker. Often, and still, stirred by restlessness, it sometimes seemed that he was trying to fill the spaces in others' lives that he was unable to fill in his own. He was good at his work, reaching people whom others found unreachable, answering worried parents in the middle of the night, leaving a family cookout to meet a student who had finally agreed to enter drug rehabilitation, piling us into the family car on a frigid Christmas Eve so that we might leave a package at a doorstep in the projects that were at the edge of our blue-collar neighborhood.

In the face of long hours and frequent economic worry, my father gave this same attention and love to my mother and to my sister and me. And yet, even with this generous and courageous spirit, he often seemed quite weary, though this tiredness was well hidden behind jovial conversation and a quick wit. As a child I could sense these textures, but as an adult I see more clearly how these wounds sometimes move beneath his skin, their life blush against the years. Watching him try to piece together a life without my mother, one that was less whole, I wondered if there is ever a time when loss becomes whole, when the fragments of memory—the lost inflection of voice, the scent of perfume that vanishes—share the moisture of our breath, so that they are at last connected by our routine, our day's life. I thought that the liminal space of the sky over ocean might make such a conversation possible with my father; but, before I could bring myself to speak, the aisles of the plane grew dark and he closed his magazine to tell me that he wished to rest, and so I returned to the protection of my work.

We spent our first days in Ireland distracted by explorations of Dublin landmarks, but after a few days of guiding our tour, I was grateful when I found myself in solitude for research and ambling in Galway. After some time apart, we reunited with cousins from Kerry for an indulgent, laughter-filled dinner on the outskirts of Salthill. In a moment of serendipity—one of those Irish coincidences while traveling that have almost become a cliché—we discovered that our waiter had grown up in Tourmakeady, the village where my grandfather was born. After calling his brother from the kitchen, the waiter quickly gave us driving directions for a more scenic route to Mayo. That moment determined our itinerary.

The next morning was soaked with the ghosts of night storms, new rain falling steadily in cold air, the mist lingering in the distance upon the Clare hills. We followed the handwritten directions on the still-damp pub napkin out of Galway City and into the solace of unvisited spaces. As we made our way to meet the stone decorum of Kylemore Abbey and the narrow roads of Connemara, we stumbled upon gates unopened into streams, lakes tumbling behind moss-edged stones. We made stops along the road, sometimes for directions, sometimes merely to observe. The darkness of slate skies was simultaneously humbling and exhilarating. Under those skies I came to appreciate the companionship of my family. In their company I tried to understand this landscape, the lavender hues fading into themselves upon the bogs, turning into the lines of a confused sky. There is a richness of color as one drives against the lake lands and bogs, a vibrancy that insinuates itself into a watcher: the colors overthrew my feeble attempts to remain a spectator. These contours engulfed me, as if to demand that I feel the experience with both body and intellect, dissolving boundaries to which I clung.

In Clifden, I walked into town with my cousin Theresa, who accompanied her father John on this trip and who, like him, seemed to feel strange out of the undiluted light and warmth of Southern California. I offered my usual excuses to skip the gift shops for a walk; to my surprise, she asked if she could join me. At the edges of the town, venturing onto a country road, we stood flat against a sheer hill that held the edge of the road in the palm of its hand. She turned to me shaking her head, saying, "People actually live here." Her wonder was coupled with a sense of impossibility; her life, back in Los Angeles, was radically disconnected from this landscape. Theresa turned to walk back to the town, but I begged a few more moments of selfish quiet. I stood with my back to the hill, considering the forces that can allow one person to find such resonance, while others do not. It had been five years since I was last in Ireland, and yet, with time and all the layers of loss that had accrued in that time, my return to this landscape was one of palpable recognition.

It is a wonder that we found the road to Tourmakeady at all. Our rental car pushed against relentless rain. The narrow roads edged by ditches held us tightly, but just as we were about to surrender to nature's forces we came upon an elderly man who was walking against the rains with astonishing ease, his coarse-coated border collie just a few steps ahead of him. By the time I convinced John—who, an hour before had taken over the wheel because he "couldn't bear to have his niece drive him around"—to stop the car so that I could bother this man for help, we were well past him, and, the road being thin, we couldn't turn around. And so I walked back down the hill, the wind nudging me forward, my boots heavy with mud. The man had a gentle but haggard expression, the layers of wind and salt sketched across the map of his skin. He knowingly looked up at me from beneath the rim of his brown hat, as if he knew this strange car filled with inexperienced Yanks would ask for assistance.

When I told him that we were looking for Tourmakeady he did not hide his surprise. He nodded and lifted his walking stick ahead of him with a promise that this was the road, and that, after climbing the hill we would find homes and a parish; that would be it. As I thanked the man and turned around I caught the edges of his mouth turn up a bit; I imagine it amused him to see how vulnerable we looked, lost in the midst of a tenacious bogland. By the time I got back to the car the rain was beginning to turn to snow, large wet flakes that reminded me of the lake snows I loved so much when living in rural New York State, just at the crosscurrents of Lake Erie and Lake Ontario. It was the kind of snow that signaled water was near, even if not in sight, as if the flakes brought some of the current and texture of the lake's depth. I got back in the car and pointed forward. My uncle nodded as he started the engine. I was beginning to learn how he wanted to communicate, and in this silence we were beginning to understand one another.

At the crest of the hill the road began to run more evenly, and, with our tank on empty, we pulled the car into T. J. O'Toole's–a general store, a pub, a fuel station, and a meeting place all at once. The proprietor told us the roads to take to the rectory house for the pastor of St. Mary's church. We expected we might find church records there, might find my grandfather's name written on paper–the veracity of an ink mark to validate his connection to a place that forty years of silence had almost erased. My father and his brother rose with new courage when we arrived at this stop. Their hesitations were replaced with a determination so unwavering that they became like schoolboys tripping over one another to escape a neighborhood prank. They were knocking on the door of the rectory residence before I even had a chance to offer them my cautious concern that we might be imposing. Before I knew it, they were waving me into the foyer of the modern ranch home, and the priest, Fr. Standún, was leading us into his firelit study straight to a large record book of handwritten entries.

My father held the book in his lap, the weight of each page falling upon his hand, and then stopped with a start when he found the entry for his father's family. He was silent for a few moments, then handed the book to John whose characteristic stern stare broke. "Jesus Christ," John said softly, "the old man left them all–three sisters and two brothers."

I watched an invisible weight lessen upon my father as he learned this, a breath released from his lungs upon finally knowing something. In this moment, decades of speculation and bafflement had, at last, been located in a factual record.

Fr. Standún told us that in the years just before my grandfather left Mayo a group of young Tourmakeady men had taken up with the nationalist cause. "They had a varied fate," he said, "but many were forced to flee." His tone made clear that those who left Ireland had the best of fates, but he was cautious not to tell more than was necessary; I think he was attuned to the fact these brothers could only bear the reality of what that parting had meant to their father through imagination, through inference.

For now, it was enough for them to know that their father had a family, that he left when only a young man. He had a history, one that would be defined by more than his own personal decision. Their father, my grandfather, had once believed in something that was dangerous to believe in, and that forced him to leave the very home he had risked his life to defend. The details of his departure are still unclear; I know that it is likely that not all of my grandfather's actions were noble, and likely that he made difficult, or even wrong decisions, decisions that would stay with him for a lifetime. But even these fragments of a narrative amounted to more than his sons had ever known of him.

As we left the rectory, my father—in a rare moment of fatherly boasting—told Fr. Standún that I studied and taught literature. At this mention, his eyes lit up; he told me that he, too, was an author and he handed me a copy of the English translation of his 1993 novel Cion Mnár (A Woman's Love). This was another surprise that we found in the rectory that day; the parish priest in this quiet village was in fact Pádraig Standún, a major figure in modern literature in Irish whose novels about love and sexuality can scandalize the pious. Nothing is simple in Tourmakeady, neither this man nor the landscape itself.

We left the rectory to find that the snow was mixed with rain, and as I took a moment to look across the distance to the church cemetery, John stopped with me. John holds an unhidden suspicion of my "overeducation," my

refuge of words and books; yet, with a bit of embarrassment, he asked me if I knew anything more about the history that may have inspired my grandfather's decision to
leave Ireland. And so, in the supple air of invading skies,
my uncle John and I had our first, and to this day, our
only, mindful conversation.

In this engagement of Ireland's land and loss, it is
impossible to remain separate from one's experience.
Much as the reality of grief sometimes separates us from
the life that surrounds us, these contours of time-marked
rock, contrasted with moss and malleable ground, would
not allow me to escape; they consumed me until I began
to see the life that comes with loss. For me, the beauty of
this landscape lay not in its green hues, not in the idylls
that so many travel narratives offer. This landscape refuses
such simplification; it is a place of layered fortitude that
cannot merely be described, but rather, must be humbly
excavated. In a time when my working hours were filled
with the self-importance of a graduate student, and when
my quiet hours were filled with the self-loathing that can
come with grief, this reminder of my own smallness
brought comfort. As I walked in the melting snow down to
the cemetery where my family rested, past crannógs,
tumbling walls, furrows, I was beginning to see the threads
that connect loss to life, to a continuum my academic
training had been urging me to sever.

At the cemetery, we began in separate corners, each
wiping the snow from the stones, looking for a familiar
name. I pulled my scarf closer and looked past its edge to
watch two weathered brothers with families of their own,
on their knees tracing the worn engravings on a stone that
read "Patrick Cusack"—inscribed evidence that their father
was once here. Their trembling hands warmed the stone:
flesh on rock. The simple act of touching the stone

seemed a prayer of recognition. Healing, for a nation or for a person sometimes comes in moments, sometimes in decades. It is in many ways a palliative process, hardly linear, rarely complete. And on this day, in the drenched air of Tourmakeady snow, some sort of healing began to unfold in the union and simultaneity with which these two middle-aged men brushed away the snow. The weight of the decades takes more than moments to lessen; but their caress of this headstone in the Mayo cemetery was a gesture of beginning.

My father and John did not know then that, just days after they returned to the States, they would bury their last brother, their father's namesake, whose too many years in asbestos-ridden Navy vessels and smoke-filled VFW halls had irreparably scarred his lungs. My father tells me now that he and his brother have decided to buy a headstone for their sister, Mary Theresa, whose grave has gone unmarked since that wooden cross that my grandfather made was taken away by groundskeepers.

John Elder, in *Reading the Mountains of Home*, writes of how at a certain point he realized that "the galvanizing stories of place are finally those we suffer for ourselves." As a scholar and teacher, I read and write of ways that verse and prose construct and reveal what I call, in my academic writing, their "mnemonic sequences," their unruly selves of war and of colonization. It hardly occurred to me that I might find the unruliness of my own broken self in these shadows.

And yet, as I read, I find that the boundary between my life and what I read grows less delineated. In "Hills" Moya Cannon asks, "Have I stooped so low as to lyricise about heather, / adjusting my love / to fit elegantly / within the terms of disinterested discourse?" I think I understand what she is trying to say; in a similar way, I am brought to question what the constructions of my academic discourse have neglected. Have I been playing the disinterested spectator in a place too vast to know?

I have an acute awareness that my family story is in no way spectacular or extraordinary. We all have stories of loss that define us; we all have stories that healing allows us to befriend, but that never dissolves the entrenched ache that we strangely grow to love. But I have come to believe that, before I can fully confront the lessons of literature, I must first be able to listen to the lessons of my own place. Like healing, this act of bridging life with reading, experience with methodology, never runs in a straight line. It is not the case that now I know how to listen and, thus, now I know how to assess. Other, more disciplined academics, who hold that scholarship should remain constantly removed and objective from private and intimate ruminations of the self, will no doubt cringe and scowl when I suggest that the personal, too, enters a scholar's work. And perhaps for such academics, the process can stay compartmentalized. For myself, though, the process is one of returns, the constant knowing and unknowing of what it means to find a dwelling place amidst the untold stories.

"Snow was general all over Ireland" observes Gabriel Conroy in "The Dead" as he unravels his wife's silenced story, "upon every part of the lonely churchyard . . . It lay thickly drifted on the crooked crosses and headstones, on the spears of the little gate, on the barren thorns." As I walked the road to the car, I wiped the last of this Tourmakeady snow from the top of a gate post, before me the snow on the headstones of St. Mary's graveyard was already disappearing.

BRIAN NERNEY

༈

STORIES FROM DOWN CELLAR

When I was a boy, my father sometimes told me family secrets: how his older brother had eloped with his high school English teacher, how one of my uncles had had his first marriage annulled, which of my mother's sisters had been pregnant when they reached the altar, and the uncle who led the charge to drop the "Mc" from McNerney in the early 1920s. My father would mimic his uncle's brogue—"I don't want to be a cop on the beat all of me life," and then add sardonically, "he dropped the Mc and sure enough he became chief of police."

Looking back, I realize that many of these stories, like those of other Irish-American families, had become secrets only in my generation. They were common knowledge to our parents or grandparents. I don't know if Irish people keep more secrets than others; it feels as if they do. I do know that I smiled in agreement when, a few years ago, I read a line in a novel that said, in Ireland, "no family worth the name is without its secret."

The first time my father told me the family murder story we were in the basement of our Dutch Colonial home built by my father's parents—Grampa Joe and Gramma Ellen—in the industrial town of Attleboro, Massachusetts. The basement, or what we called "down cellar," was dry and the concrete walls and floor were painted blue-gray. Standing at the bottom of the stairs, I could see my mother's laundry, the black-and-white octopus furnace, my father's workbench, some old wooden shelves loaded with canned goods, two rows of bookshelves and, next to them, a locked white metal cabinet where my father kept our guns. Whenever my father unlocked the gun cabinet, he stood by it like a guard, controlling the movement of each rifle or pistol as if it were a precious gem.

One Saturday afternoon when I was eleven, and we were supposed to be out raking leaves, my father and I were down cellar with the gun cabinet open. I spotted a shiny revolver with a black handle that he had never shown me. "What's that pistol on the top shelf?" I asked.

"It's nickel-plated, .38-caliber," Dad said. "I bought it from Ted White up the street when I was eighteen." He held its tan leather holster in his right hand and slipped the gun out with his left, and, as was his habit when removing or replacing a gun from the cabinet, he pushed the cylinder open with his index finger and checked to see that it was empty. As he closed the cylinder, he turned the revolver over in his hands, studying it as if it were a family heirloom.

"When I got home with this," my father said, "my mother was standing at the stove cooking dinner. She had seen lots of guns, but when I drew this revolver out of its holster, she blanched, clutched the back of a kitchen chair and eased herself onto the wooden seat. She said, 'Sit down, Jim; I have something to tell you.

'One day when I was thirteen, my oldest sister had a row with her husband. He accused her of adultery. She had done nothing of the kind and demanded that he apologize, that he give back her good name. When he refused, she threw him out. I heard about all this when I went over to her apartment. We were sitting in the kitchen having tea when her husband came back with a gun he bought that afternoon, just like the one you've got there. He came right in and shot my sister twice, point-blank, and killed her. He pointed the gun at me but it misfired.

'I was the only eyewitness and I testified against him. He was convicted and they executed him at Sing Sing in the electric chair. When the doctors did the autopsy, they found a brain tumor the size of a golf ball, so he must have been crazy.'"

I was completely surprised by what my father told me. I said nothing, just looked back and forth between his face and his hands, his long fingers extending over much of the short-barreled gun.

"The story hit me like a punch in the gut," Dad said. "I'd never heard a thing about it."

"Jeez, Dad," I said, "it's just like the movies." The courtroom scene from *To Kill a Mocking Bird* popped into my head.

"She was brave," he said, "testifying when just a girl. It must have been very frightening. But she was tough. I couldn't believe she had kept the secret all those years."

My father opened and closed the cylinder of the revolver to see that it was empty, then slipped the gun back into the holster and shoved it back up on the high shelf. He quickly locked the cabinet door. The conversation was over.

———

Before he was ravaged by Parkinson's Disease, my father was a good storyteller. I listened uncritically to his accounts of his boyhood experiments with explosives, his tyrannical mother, and his service in the Navy during World War II. But as I grew older I began to recognize that the family murder story was a cleaned-up version of the real events. In his later years, he sometimes ended this favorite family tale with the line, "The New York City newspapers covered the story." It was as if he had said to me, "Go to the newspapers if you want to read about our family's miseries."

One spring break, seven years after my father died, I took up his challenge by scouring the early years of the New York Times. At that time they were available only on microfilm, and housed in the basement of the university library. I had found a list of criminals who had been executed in the electric chair at Sing Sing prison, just north of New York City. Using the list of names as a guide, I began reading the stories of the death row inmates, slogging through gruesome reports of murders and executions for three-and-a-half days. I almost skipped a story dated October 5, 1891, because the headline did not square with what my father had told to me—the story he had heard from his mother, Ellen Murphy, the youngest of the seven Murphy children.

But then, paragraph two: "A little sister of Mrs. Osmond's, Ellen Murphy, a girl of thirteen years, was present and witnessed" the events.

My god, I thought, That's Gramma Ellen! This is the story! I flushed with excitement. I was shocked by the difference between the family story and the truth; my hands and feet tingled. I read the story again and then did a little dance around my chair before yanking the tape out of the machine and running to the copying service.

I had expected that searching the newspapers would be fun, like piecing together the clues in crime fiction.

But what I learned from the newspaper reports, and later, from a transcript of the trial stored in the library at the John Jay College of Criminal Justice, was not the entertaining family story I had heard from my father and then repeated so often myself. The written sources revealed that some of my family members were violent and abusive.

My father's grandparents—Patrick Murphy and Catherine Congdon Murphy—emigrated from Ireland in 1860, with a little education and a little savings. Patrick was born in 1840 to Andrew Murphy and Mary Walsh Murphy in a rented farmhouse in the townland of Ballynamuck, near Churchtown, North Cork. He survived the Famine; his village did not. My great-grandfather and many of his thirteen siblings survived to age fourteen and became apprentices, several of them in shoemaking and related trades. Patrick's brother William, for instance, is listed as a shoemaker in an 1880 business directory for the city of Cork.

Catherine Congdon was born to a land-owning family in a nearby town. Patrick and Catherine grew up in Ireland's vibrant oral culture. Catherine's home may well have been visited by shanachies, and Patrick's cobbler shop was a center for swapping gossip and arguing local politics. When Patrick and Catherine, along with other family members, sailed to New York City just before the Civil War, Patrick—who had apprenticed to a shoemaker—arrived as a full-fledged artisan.

They moved into an apartment in Kip's Bay, just below midtown Manhattan between First and Second Avenues, and as it turned out they remained in the neighborhood for the rest of their lives. Patrick Murphy opened his boot-making business on Second Avenue among other small shops, houses, three-story tenements and open lots. After New York City built the elevated railway in 1878 on

Second and Third Avenues, my entrepreneurial great-grandfather moved his shop to the corner of Third Avenue and 38th Street. Regular customers could easily access his shop, and people passing to and from the steps up to the El could look in his windows to see samples of his specialty—ladies dress boots in soft, hand-sewn leather. This off-the-El location placed his shop at the intersection of two neighborhoods, Kips' Bay to the east of Third Avenue and Murray Hill to the West. Kip's Bay was the tougher neighborhood, with tenements, slaughterhouses, bars, brothels, and warehouses along the East River and First Avenue; the more upscale Murray Hill included department stores, small apartment buildings, brownstones, and mansions for such families as the Astors and Morgans. Gentlemen from Murray Hill and artisans from Kip's Bay could all join the conversation about Tammany Hall politics and stories of the old country in his shop. But though these differing worlds coverged in his shop, my great-grandfather had no wish to stay in the raffish environs of Kip's Bay.

Patrick's knowledge of bootmaking fueled his ambition. His youngest daughter Ellen once recalled how in the late 1880s her father was making an entry in his accounts book because "he was after making a gift of a pair of boots to a gentleman." It was a sort of bet: if he placed a pair of well-made boots in the hands of a wealthy gentleman, then that gentleman and his rich friends would order boots for their wives and daughters.

Patrick Murphy strove for both financial success and respectability. On Sunday mornings, my great-grandparents would stroll down Fifth Avenue after attending Mass at the new Saint Patrick's Cathedral. They slowly worked their way south along the broad sidewalks, greeting many of the hundreds of other city dwellers dressed in their Sunday best. Catherine in her high-necked dress and brightly colored hat smiled to passersby, while Patrick tipped his silk top hat. A tall, slender man with a dark full beard, Patrick knew the rich and famous in a special way. As a maker of dress boots and the proprietor of his own shop, he worked at the top of the artisan's hierarchy. When he tipped his top hat, his muscular, stained hand against the black silk hat signaled in one brief gesture both his craft and his desire for respectability. Moderate in his eating and drinking habits, he worked hard, assimilated to American life and could fairly be called successful by his forties.

Like many immigrant families, Patrick and Catherine Murphy took in boarders. One was a young man named John Osmond, who was short, thin, and wore a cap. Osmond fell in love with the Murphy's eldest daughter, Mamie, who was, in the language of the time, a "handsome woman." Talkative and socially adept, she loved to attend plays and concerts, which she could afford because she was one of New York City's early telephone operators. Osmond, who earned modest wages as a brass polisher, also liked to dominate conversations, and bought tickets to theaters only to please Mamie.

After more than two years of courtship, Mamie and Osmond married at St. Stephen's Church on February 15, 1885. Mamie's youngest sister, Ellen, aged six, was the youngest of the Osmonds and Murphys in attendance. The celebration was small; Catherine, Patrick's wife of more than twenty-five years and the mother of Mamie, Ellen and five other siblings, had died of consumption just a year before.

In the transcript of the trial, the Osmond family and their friends remembered John Osmond and Mamie

Murphy as a loving couple who did many things together–
going to plays and concerts, fishing in various locations
around New York City. They remembered them quar-
relling occasionally, but making up within a few days.

My family, the Murphys, remembered things very dif-
ferently. They recalled Mamie and Osmond as happy for
the first ten months while they lived with the Murphys.
But once they moved into a two-room apartment of their
own, they recalled that Osmond began to drink heavily,
became abusive, and skipped work for long stretches. It
increasingly fell to Mamie's family to support her.

While boarding with the Murphys, Osmond had seen
my great-grandfather insist on such domestic details as a
clean dinner napkin every day. But Osmond failed to recognize that his father-in-law could be so demanding
because was also an ambitious and steady provider. Once
Osmond and Mamie had their own place, he grew tyrannical. If his supper were not ready on time, Osmond
slapped Mamie across the face. On one occasion, when
Osmond could not force Mamie to give him ten dollars
from the household money–which he wanted for liquor–
Osmond pushed her onto their bed and bit into her right
breast so viciously that she had to go the doctor. Mamie
sometimes overpowered the smaller Osmond, but mostly
she castigated him with her sharp tongue. Mamie's
youngest sister, Ellen, remembered how on Easter Sunday,
1889, she went up to where Mamie and Osmond were living at 708 Third Avenue. Mamie had two black eyes.
When young Ellen asked what happened, Mamie would
only sob and shake her head. After a few moments,
Mamie said, "I may have to leave him." Osmond, lying
drunk on the bed in the next room, heard what Mamie
said and came roaring into the kitchen, grabbed Mamie by

the throat and growled, "Young lady, I'll empty my revolver in you yet."

Shocked and confused, Ellen ran home. She reported Osmond's threat to her father, who tried to soothe her fears and promised to talk with Mamie and Osmond. My great-grandfather swore her to secrecy so as to keep it within the family.

After five years of marriage Mamie and Osmond were childless. They quarreled bitterly. Osmond drank heavily and worked only sporadically. During the early months of 1890, Mamie struck up a relationship with one of Osmond's cousins, John Burchell who owned a four-story house at 609 Third Avenue. A steady, hard-working man who wore a bowler hat when he stepped out, Burchell lived alone in a four-room apartment on the top floor of the house. Mamie saw an opportunity. She agreed to cook and keep house in lieu of rent, and moved herself and Osmond in with Burchell.

Ellen, aged twelve at the time, wore smocked dresses and fresh brown curls, and looked every bit the proper young lady. Yet she was street savvy. She knew how to avoid meat-packers as they stumbled out of bars, the gangs of kids who roamed up Second Avenue, and the fast-moving horses and carriages of the rich as they sped from Murray Hill. She was proud to run errands for her older sister, and having learned housekeeping after their mother's death, she helped Mamie clean, organize and decorate her modest apartment. During the summer of 1891, she and Mamie made six hanging bird cages and bought parakeets to fill them, imitating what wealthy people in Murray Hill and other upscale neighbor-hoods had been doing for several decades.

Throughout the summer of 1891, Osmond came and went. Mamie threw him out for drunkenness several times.

Burchell went to work every day and enjoyed Mamie's company after dinner each evening. Patrick Murphy had no immediate reasons to fear for his daughter. When Osmond and Mamie's quarrels exploded into threats and abuse, Ellen ran to the corner for a policeman.

On July 15, 1891, reinforcements moved onto the scene when Patrick Murphy persuaded Ellen and Mamie's middle sister, Kate, and her husband Peter O'Brien to move into an apartment on the third floor of Burchell's house. With Kate and Peter on the third floor, and Ellen living with Mamie and Burchell, my great-grandfather thought he had created a respectable house at 609 Third Avenue. Patrick must have thought that the presence of Ellen, who turned thirteen on August 18, would maintain propriety between Mamie and Burchell. He hoped any quarrels and romances would be kept private.

But on Labor Day, Osmond, who had recently rented a furnished room on Second Avenue, came to collect a trunk full of his belongings. Osmond recalled in court that when he entered the apartment, Burchell was in the kitchen and Mamie was napping in her bed. Osmond went out to the front room and began to fill his trunk with clothes. Mamie dressed herself and came out to the parlor. According to the transcript of the trial, Osmond claimed that he tried to reason with his wife.

"Mamie will you come live with me?" asked Osmond. "I have got a hundred dollars offered to me now to start housekeeping."

"Oh," Mamie said, "where would you get a hundred dollars?"

"My brother offered it to me."

Mamie looked around the apartment. "What is the matter with this home?"

"You know what's the matter with it."

"Can't you live here?" she said.

"What for, to be a cloak for you and Burchell?"

Mamie began pulling Osmond's clothes out of drawers and off hooks and tossing them into the trunk. "I'll never live with you again," she declared. "Get out. Take all your things out. I want you to get out of here."

"Mamie, you know we once lived together like two doves. But this past year was hell on earth, and it's all your doings with Burchell," said Osmond. "I caught you in bed with Burchell twice. You expect a husband to bear that? And now you're putting me out when I know this thing exists between you and Burchell." He stepped toward Mamie for one more attempt.

"You come with me and I will forgive all of that," Osmond said.

"No," Mamie said, "not after the way you've treated me."

"All right, that settles it," Osmond said, and he slammed down the lid of the trunk. The loud bang brought Burchell out from the kitchen into the front room.

"John Burchell, remember now," Osmond shouted, "you have taken my wife out, you have been in bed with my wife, you have cooed and loved and hugged right before my very eyes. Now remember, my wife has ordered me out. This is your home, not mine, but if you keep my wife here I will come pull her out or there will be some trouble." Osmond bent forward, grabbed a handle on the end of the trunk and pulled it off the sofa and up onto his back. He teetered toward the door, got his balance when he grabbed the door knob with his left hand and flung the door open. He looked back at Burchell. "You keep her here under your roof and against my wishes."

"There's a home here for us all," Burchell said. "And I don't see any harm in taking Mamie and her family out to the beach or to the theater."

"As her husband, I order you to put her out," Osmond said. "You are keeping her under your roof." Straining under the weight of the trunk, Osmond kept after Burchell.

"I want this thing to stop," Osmond said. "You're only creating a scandal."

The appeal to respectability from a drunken abuser surprised Burchell. "I don't know what you are talking about," Burchell said. Burchell walked past him and down the stairs.

Osmond later claimed in court that he pulled his trunk up on his back and went quietly downstairs and left the house. But in court, Kate O'Brien, the sister who lived on the third floor, testified that she heard Osmond, Mamie, and Burchell shouting at one another before Osmond came down with his trunk on his back. "When he got to the bottom of the stairs," Kate recalled, "he turned back and called my sister a vile name—called her a whore." The enormity of Osmond's offense, shouting out such an insult, was clear to Kate. "That," she said in closing her testimony, "was the cause of the divorce."

Kate's story is similar to what Ellen—who approached the house as Osmond was leaving—recalled. Ellen testified that Osmond stopped on the sidewalk and shouted up at the windows for all the neighbors to hear, "You're a whore to him. Nothing but a common whore."

When she told her father what happened, he was furious. Ellen had never before seen her father so angry, never seen anything wound his pride as deeply as when Osmond called Mamie a whore in public. Within three weeks, Mamie, with financial and moral support from her father and from Burchell, filed suit for divorce and alimony. The grounds were cruel and inhuman treatment.

In court, Ellen testified that the pending divorce so infuriated and humiliated Osmond that he kept coming around the apartment, harassing Mamie one time and then another time pleading with her to come live with him.

"Won't you come and live with me in my furnished room?" Osmond asked only a day after he was served with the divorce papers.

"Will you give back my good name that you have taken away before everyone in this neighborhood?" replied Mamie.

He refused and badgered Mamie and then Burchell to give back his fishing knife and his pistol. They both refused. Osmond worked a few days and saved $3.50. He later testified that he was so jealous of Burchell and so disturbed by the thought of losing Mamie through divorce that on the Thursday before the first court date, he went to a pawn shop and bought a .38-caliber, nickel-plated revolver loaded with new cartridges.

On the night of October 3, 1891, only two days before Mamie's lawyer was to begin the divorce proceedings, Osmond coolly and calmly shot Mamie and Burchell as they sat with Ellen at their kitchen table eating steamed clams and beer. Ellen was the only eyewitness. Osmond was arrested Sunday morning at his brother's apartment by officers Bernard Malarkey and Robert Deming. He confessed to the officers on the way to the station and wrote out a confession for a Captain Ryan, one of New York's legendary police officers in his day.

Because Osmond had confessed, the district attorney advised my great-grandfather that Osmond's attorneys would use an insanity defense to get Osmond life in prison.

As soon as Patrick Murphy learned this, he began coaching thirteen-year-old Ellen. He wanted to be certain her story would persuade a jury to convict Osmond of intentional, premeditated, first-degree murder. He rehearsed questions three or four times a week with his youngest daughter, knowing she would be frightened when she faced Osmond in court. And based on the transcript of the trial, Ellen was indeed cool and calm throughout her testimony, even when defense attorneys peppered her with questions.

In contrast to Ellen's crisp, articulate testimony, Osmond rambled on for several hours, remembering minute details until the moment of the shooting and then claiming lapses of memory. His own recollections of minutiae undercut his insanity defense, and the defense was further discredited by a medical expert who testified that he knew of no such "nervous or mental disease." The jury took less than an hour to find Osmond guilty of first-degree murder. One week later, Judge Ingraham sentenced Osmond to death in the electric chair at Sing Sing.

Ellen's performance reflects something we do not see in the movies: how much good coaching it takes to develop a child witness. Given the speed with which the jury returned the conviction that Patrick Murphy wanted, he achieved his goal: my great-grandfather employed the courts—and his youngest daughter—to bring about justice. They did the right thing and they were honorable people, perhaps heroes, for having done so.

Ellen sat through enough of the jury selection and the trial to know that conviction for first-degree murder meant capital punishment, but I wonder if my great-grandfather explained capital punishment—execution—to her in detail during the coaching sessions. In late 1891 and early 1892, the newspapers, which he was fond of reading to his family, reported several bungled attempts to execute criminals in the new electric chair at Sing Sing. I suspect that my great-grandfather did not read those pieces aloud to his family after dinner, in order to spare young Ellen a full knowledge of the implications of her testimony.

Osmond appealed his sentence. During the year that Osmond was pleading for his life, Ellen turned fourteen and found a job in the book department at Macy's department store. On June 12, she probably went to work and returned home tired. I have often wondered if, that evening after dinner, my great-grandfather, proud of having coached Ellen so well and having secured justice and revenge, rested his arm on the icebox and read the news to the family. *The New York Times* reported that John Osmond had walked to the death chamber carrying a brass crucifix and murmuring, "Save us, O Lord. I repent of my sins. Save us, O Lord." The autopsy revealed no physical abnormalities. There was no brain tumor, no physical proof he was "crazy" as Gramma Ellen would later claim.

And what about the following day? Could my great-grandfather contain his pride when he read the following editorial in the *New York Times*:

> It is worth noting the entire lack of especial interest in the execution of the murderer John Osmond at Sing Sing yesterday. It was quietly and efficiently performed by the electric process, and death was declared by the surgeons to have been instantaneous. This method of administering capital punishment is now accepted generally as the swiftest, surest and most satisfactory yet invented, and condemnation of it has practically ceased among intelligent men.

Patrick Murphy must have counted himself among those "intelligent men." Until Mamie was killed, his concern over respectability apparently was greater than his concern for Mamie and Ellen's safety. Or perhaps he confused the two and hoped in some unrealistic way that his efforts at respectability also would protect Mamie and Ellen.

My great-grandfather calculated the effect of Ellen's courtroom testimony, her telling of the story, with the precision that comes from having lived in a culture rich in storytelling. But my great-grandfather did not calculate, did not imagine—and perhaps no person could imagine under such circumstances—the long-term effects of placing Ellen at the center of this drama, and insisting she be dispassionate in her telling.

Ellen, my grandmother, grew up to be a harsh, despotic person, which I cannot help but speculate was a consequence of being cast in the role of a star witness at age thirteen. What we do know is that when she told the story in later life, she sanitized it, deleting the abuse, the divorce, the love affair, and Burchell's death. More important, the account she told her children insisted that Osmond was insane, an alteration that unraveled the compelling theme of her own testimony—that Osmond was cool and calculating while murdering Mamie and Burchell. Ellen loved Mamie and she never forgave Osmond for shooting her sister in cold blood. But it is hard not to conclude that Ellen wanted to shed the responsibility for having sent Osmond to the electric chair.

———

My research into my family began as an almost whimsical investigation, a curiosity about the facts. But it continues as a vein of deep experience that prompts me to contemplate such topics as abuse, desire, revenge, and also the power of storytelling. Researching my family history in libraries, museums, cemeteries, and the Irish countryside has been the discovery of a reality that shaped my family's history and portions of my character. Discovering these qualities in family research has given my research a weight, texture, and feel comparable to my experience of the natural world; my family research has turned out to be like Thoreau's activity at his cabin by Walden Pond, which he referred to in Walden as confronting the "hard bottom and rocks in place, which we can call reality."

In 2002, long after my father had died and a year or more after uncovering the facts behind the family murder story, I was visiting my 85-year-old mother in Massachusetts, and told her during dinner of my discovery and my plans to disclose the whole story.

Rapping her knuckles on the table, she said, "If your father were alive, he would not want you writing about it."

"Dad kept the duplicate pistol all his life and liked telling the story," I said. "And besides, I think he added that line about the New York City newspapers covering the story so that I could find the facts. I think he hoped that I would tell the story."

"Not on your life," she said out of the corner of her mouth. Then she turned on me. "You don't air dirty laundry in public.

"Your father worked so hard to do things right, to get an education, to earn some respect. He detested those old lies about the Irish, always drunk, beating on each other and whoring around." She took a sip from her Manhattan, put the glass on the table and rolled the stem between her fingers while she glared at me.

"Mom, Dad is dead. I can write about it now," I said.

My mother's eyes filled with tears. She dabbed her eyes with her napkin. She picked up her fork and tried to finish her dinner.

I watched my mother trying not to cry. I kept quiet and ate my chicken and rice. I felt ashamed. Through research I had developed empathy for five dead ancestors, but I had talked to my mother as if I were ignorant of my parents' passionate love for one another.

Later that evening, I was down cellar sitting at my father's desk, which was partially surrounded by shelves full of his books. My mother, despite arthritis and debilitating back pain, worked her way down cellar. Dressed in her dark blue robe and slippers, she slowly made herself comfortable in a burgundy, winged-back chair opposite where I was sitting, looking though some old family photographs.

"Your father knew the truth," she said. "One time, after the war, in the early '50s, your father and I went to a convention in New York City. One afternoon we took a cab over to the New York Public Library and a librarian helped your father find the story in the *Times*. I waited in the reading room while he went into the newspaper room, so I didn't see the story. Anyway, he came out after a while and said, 'I've seen enough. Let's go.' And that," she said, her voice rising a little and her hands turning upward, "was all he ever said about it."

She lowered her hands and in a calm, lower register said, "He never spoke of it again except to repeat the story we all know." Her voice signaled that she accepted my father's decision to repeat only the sanitized version of the story.

I flashed back to the day down cellar when my father first told me the story and held the nickel-plated revolver in his long fingers. As I recalled the scene, I searched the fleeting memory of my father's face and saw only signs of caring and concern. But my mother's story had caused the value of that day down cellar to collapse like a bridge into a river. What had been a moment of truth, of feeling grown up, became one of evasion, of feeling like a little boy. "Mom," I asked, "if Dad knew the truth, why didn't he tell the whole story?"

"I think he was ashamed," she said. She looked at me as if I were a bit daft. "Brian, he was part of a big Irish family. People could be brutal. And just for that reason, your grandmother never told the whole story either." My mother pulled herself up to the edge of the chair and leveled her gaze at me. "If you tell the whole story, it's yours, the whole messy business. But remember," she said, pausing for dramatic effect, "your father kept those ugly details to himself all those years." She glared at me, then pushed herself up out of the wing-backed chair, her hands shaking under her own weight. She shuffled in her fleece-lined slippers toward the door.

I felt bewildered. I was surrounded by my father's books, but they could not tell me what I wanted to know. I wanted him back more than ever. I wanted to talk with him honestly about the abuse, love affair, divorce, coaching, testimony and capital punishment.

"But, damn it, why didn't he tell you? Why didn't he tell me?"

"I'm not sure, dear," my mother said without turning around. "Maybe he wanted to protect us from life's suffering."

Redefinitions

BRIGITTINE M. FRENCH

∾

"WE'RE ALL IRISH":
TRANSFORMING IRISH IDENTITY
IN A MIDWESTERN COMMUNITY

With a solemn air, my grandmother Mary B. O'Neill told me, "When you ride in a parade, you have to wave the right way" as she slowly demonstrated her instructions.[1] With all the possible earnestness of a five-year-old, I internalized the "correct" wave and performed it to perfection when I accompanied the local homecoming queen in a 1976 parade. Both the parade and my small role in it, as the "junior attendant," were ritualized annual performances in Everly, Iowa, a rural farming community of approximately 800 people of European-American descent situated in the northwest corner of the state. But, the image of my young self perched on the back of a convertible in a long velvet dress waving exactly as I had been instructed falls horribly short in my memory, particularly because my grandmother did not witness it. She died unexpectedly, a few days after the last advice she gave me. I never had the opportunity to ask her how she knew about proper parade etiquette, or why she insisted that my

1. My colleague Douglas Caulkins and I conducted research in O'Neill, Nebraska, with Grinnell College anthropology students. Students Ilana Meltzer and Molly Offer-Westort collected data during the 2005 St. Patrick's Day Weekend. Aric Pearson spent six weeks in O'Neill during the summer of 2005 conducting fieldwork and interviewing local residents about Irish identity through grant support from the National Science Foundation Grant BCS-0217156, Douglas Caulkins and Carol Trosset, principle investigators. Grinnell College provided support for our collective faculty and student research through the Mentor Advanced Project.

dress for the occasion be a green one. It is only recently, as an adult following the scholarly path of the anthropologist, that I have been led to weave together the threads of my grandmother's life with issues of memory, culture, and Irish identity in Midwestern America.

My grandmother, Mary O'Neill, born in 1918, knew about parade etiquette because—as I discovered after piecing together the rarely mentioned event in my family—she appeared in one. The parade she participated in was not just any local celebration, the kind that is a common cultural practice in rural communities in the Midwest. She was, in fact, an invited guest at the historic inaugural festivities of the St. Patrick's Day celebration in O'Neill Nebraska, in 1967. As many of her seven daughters recounted when I began to ask questions, and as family photos illustrating fragments of the grand event confirmed, my grandmother had set off for an eight-hour car trip from northwest Iowa to her native Nebraska with all her finery and a twinkle in her eye to celebrate her Irish heritage in the town of O'Neill. She traveled to the newly proclaimed "Irish Capital of Nebraska" to remember her Irishness publicly together with some 5,000 others who had gathered for the event.[2] The archives of the local newspaper, the Holt County Independent, further reveal that Mrs. Mary O'Neill Wilbur was honored in the parade—following a banquet—as a direct descendant of the town's flamboyant founder General John O'Neill, former president of the Fenian Brotherhood in the United States.[3]

My grandmother's experience of Irishness in O'Neill occurred during a moment when conceptions of Irish identity in the Midwestern United States and elsewhere

2. *Holt County Independent,* 23 March 1967.
3. *Holt County Independent,* 23 March 1967.

were shifting dramatically. Notions of Irish identity have undergone substantial transformations from the mid-1800s to our own time; examining her experience provides a vehicle for tracking the changes in these conceptions. Three specific moments stand out: first, the founding and initial settlement of O'Neill, Nebraska; second, the development of St. Patrick's Day activities in the community and the concomitant emergence of a self-consciously "ethnic" identity there; and third, the contemporary notion of Irish identity as an explicitly de-ethnicized construct, displayed in service of an unmarked, local, white American identity.

These shifting conceptions of Irishness hinged on notions of collectivity that also underwent significant changes. Briefly, Irish identity in O'Neill, Nebraska, during the late 1800s was grounded in collective experiences of "exile" invoked through a named peoplehood—the Irish.[4] Less than a century later, Irishness became an identity based upon individual experiences. In this ontological shift from Irish peoplehood to Irish ethnicity, women like my grandmother played a key role in its performative invocations. In the early twenty-first century, Irishness was once again recollectivized in O'Neill in such a manner that the locally prevailing ideology asserts "everyone can be Irish." The identity no longer requires any substantive cultural, political, or even familial bonds. Instead, Irish identity is now being reclaimed as a corporate identity—one defined by local place, irrespective of one's ethnic origins, and conceived as an integral part of broader national conceptions of collective Americanness.

---

4. The construction of Irish emigration as "exile" was a pervasive trope in the nineteenth century. The concept is definitively examined in Kerby Miller, *Emigrants and Exiles: Ireland and the Irish Exodus to North America* (New York: Oxford University Press, 1985). See also *The Exiles of Erin: Nineteenth-Century Irish-American Fiction*, ed. Charles Fanning (Pennsylvania, Dufour Editions, 1997).

The officially commemorated history of the town begins with the Irish colonization of the local prairie led by General John J. O'Neill (1834–1878). While local monuments and histories of the town highlight the particularities of General O'Neill's settlement, it must also be understood as part of the larger historical trend of self-consciously Irish colonization projects in the Midwestern United States undertaken from the 1850s to the 1880s. According to one pioneering Catholic clergyman, Father De Smet, at the time of its settlement in 1854 there was not another permanent town or village of whites in the entire Nebraska territory.[5] After the locally forgotten forcible removal of American Indian populations to Kansas in the same year, Reverend Jeremiah Tracey led a party of sixty Irish Catholics from the settlement of Garry Owen, Iowa, to Dakota County in northeastern Nebraska. There, Irish Catholics made one of the first settlements of European-Americans in Nebraska.[6] Indeed, several colonization projects directed toward relocating Irish immigrants by their fellow Irish, directed by both clergy and lay persons, were part of an ongoing movement explicitly designed to ameliorate the deplorable social and economic conditions of Irish immigrants living in densely populated Eastern seaboard cities.[7] In this historical context, Irishness, from the initial arrival of white Europeans in Nebraska, was intimately tied to collective experiences of exile from Ireland and to the dire circumstances in

5. Sister Mary Evangela Henthorne, *The Irish Catholic Colonization Association of the United States* (Champaign: Twin City Printing Company, 1932), p. 132.
6. Henthorne, p. 132.
7. Henthorne, pp. 20–23 discusses several such projects, including the Charitable Irish Society of Boston in 1737, the Hibernian Society for the Relief of Emigrants from Ireland in 1790, the Irish Emigrant Society in 1841, the Hibernian Benevolent Society in Chicago in 1848, and the Irish Catholic Colonization Association founded in 1879.

which they found themselves in the major cities of the United States before they reached the prairie.

It was both the aspiration of improving the plight of the Irish immigrant and an overt political commitment to Irish independence from Britain that General John O'Neill marshaled to settle one community on the Nebraska prairie. Turning to the specifics of the polemic and memorialized history of General O'Neill, one is struck by how emblematic of the history of Irish immigration to the United States the early life of the town's founder appears. Born in the North of Ireland in 1834, John O'Neill lost his father at an early age. Soon afterward, his mother, with three children under the age of five, left for the United States—part of the migration of some two million Irish people during the thirty years from 1830 to 1865.[8] John, who was initially left in the care of his grandfather, joined his mother in New Jersey in 1848 at age fourteen, during the height of the Famine.[9]

O'Neill became passionately involved in the Fenian Brotherhood, an involvement that colored his vision for potential Irish immigrants to his colony in Nebraska. Formally organized in 1858, the Fenian movement carried a fundamental commitment to political, financial, and military action for the purpose of gaining the independence of Ireland.[10] O'Neill, and thousands of other Fenians, gained substantial military experience when they fought in the Union army. One historian observes, "With the end of the American Civil War in April, 1865, came the mustering out of the thousands of Irish-Americans who had fought in it. The contributions of the Fenians both in officers and men was notable. . . .

8. Mabel Gregory Walker, *The Fenian Movement* (Colorado Springs: Ralph Myles Publisher, 1969), p. vii.

9. Gerald R. Noonan, "A Characterization of General John O'Neill in Light of His Colonizing Efforts in the State of Nebraska, 1872–1878," M. A. thesis, (St. Paul Seminary, St. Paul: Minnesota, 1961).

10. William D'Arcy, *The Fenian Movement in the United States 1858–1886* (Washington: Catholic University of America, 1947), p. 15.

11. D'Arcy, p. 61.

Besides the active Fenians there were enrolled in the Union Armies about 200,000 Irish."[11] They hoped to capitalize on their military experiences and on anti-British sentiment in the United States to mobilize for Irish independence.

John O'Neill zealously and dutifully delivered that hope. On May 22, 1868, the Fenian command ordered O'Neill and his Thirteenth Infantry to Buffalo, New York, the strategic base for the planned invasion of Canada. Under the protection of darkness, O'Neill led approximately 800 men across the Niagara River on May 31 and successfully occupied the Canadian village of Fort Erie. Despite an initial success against a column of Canadian volunteers at the Battle of Ridgeway, an American gunboat prevented the Fenians that remained in Buffalo from providing reinforcements and supplies. Although O'Neill was arrested by American officials after retreating across the border, he was not dissuaded by this setback.[12] Instead, he continued to pursue the cause of Irish independence, while rising in the organization with a promotion to the rank of brigadier general, from which his title derives. Soon afterward, O'Neill was elected president of the organization on January 1, 1868.[13] O'Neill subsequently led an additional two failed attacks on Canada in 1870 and 1871, which once again landed him in federal custody.[14]

When O'Neill realized he would not be permitted to continue his military assaults on the Canadian front, he turned his attention to the Western frontier and to the new project of encouraging his fellow Irish immigrants out of the squalid conditions in Eastern mines and cities. As an individual social actor participating in the larger social trend to better the conditions of recent immigrants from Ireland,

12. Noonan, p. 3.
13. D'Arcy, p. 279.
14. Noonan, p. 4.

O'Neill traveled up and down the East Coast recruiting Irish men and women to colonize the Nebraska prairie. O'Neill endeavored to "build up a young Ireland on the virgin prairies of Nebraska and there rear a monument more lasting than granite or marble to the Irish."[15] The social and economic processes of Irish immigration to the Midwestern United States were thus intimately tied to the shared experience of developing new communities in "exile" from Ireland through colonizing efforts directed by, and undertaken for, a named collective Irish people.

John O'Neill further politicized the project by linking it to the struggle for Irish independence from Britain. He based both commitments, to economic betterment and Irish independence, upon a presumed notion of collective Irish identity:

> I had a double object in encouraging our people to emigrate from the overcrowded cities and states of the east to settle upon the cheap and free lands of the west. The first was that they might better their own condition and that of their families and the second was that they might be in a position, from their improved circumstances and their nearness to the contemplated field of future operations, to assist the cause of Irish liberty.[16]

The success of one project in the homeland would be facilitated by the other on the prairie. When O'Neill brought thirteen men, two women, and five children to the Elkhorn valley of Holt County, Nebraska, in 1874, he clearly believed that the practice of developing new Irish

15. John O'Neill to Bishop James O'Connor, 27 December 1876 Onahan Scrapbook, cited in Henthorne.
16. John O'Neill, "The Founding of O'Neill," *O'Neill Frontier*, 7 August 1924, cited in Noonan, p. 9.

settlements could advance the cause of Irish freedom in the homeland. O'Neill and those few immigrants were joined by a common perception of exile from Ireland that grounded their collective identities as Irish.

Capitalizing upon this transnational, collective notion of peoplehood, O'Neill asserted that Irish colonization in the Midwest was:

> The next best thing to fighting for Ireland. I shall continue at it despite every obstacle until called upon for sterner work when I will be found where an O'Neill properly belongs—which is not so much in talking about Ireland's wrongs, as in fighting for Ireland's rights. . . . We do not intend to forget the cause of Ireland but, desire to be in a better position to serve it when the opportunity presents. The prairies are wide and there is plenty of room for drill and instruction, and there is no law against shooting deer and antelope, in season which will be very good practice—until we can find other game.[17]

One can assume that everyone in the audience understood exactly what target the general meant by "other game." Despite his rhetorical zeal, the materiality of O'Neill's plans for his fellow countrymen and women in Nebraska was as fraught as his invasions of Canada.

Like some other Irish immigrant colonists brought to the agrarian Midwest, the first group of O'Neill's settlers found open prairie and little else to sustain them upon arrival. They initially built a small sod shelter to protect themselves from the elements and were soon joined by a

17 John O'Neill, Public Address given at Head Quarters of O'Neill's Irish American Colonies, (no publisher: Philadelphia, 1876).
18. Henthorne, The Irish Catholic Colonization Association of the United States, p. 137.

second colony of about a dozen men, some with families, in 1875.[18] In 1876, the largest group, 102 men and a
few women and children, arrived in O'Neill, while only
five of the original Irish immigrants remained in the
community.[19] While the immigrants battled poor soil,
drought, grasshopper plagues, and a lack of infrastruc-
ture, they remained committed to their Catholic faith. A
committee commissioned a local carpenter to build a
church that was completed in July, 1877. The Irish-born
Father John T. Smith said the first Mass and remained in
the community as the first permanent clergy of St.
Joseph's Parish.[20] With an incipient Irish Catholic community in place, General O'Neill endeavored to recruit
more Irish colonists, but fate worked against him. While
traveling east to promote his settlement, O'Neill fell ill
and died in Omaha, on January 18, 1878.

Although the general was laid to rest, the town he
founded grew and transformed. By 1882, the town of
O'Neill had become the county seat, and the administra-
tive and commercial center for grain and cattle-raising in
the area.[21] A major aspect of this change was the shift
away from a distinctively identifiable Irish population. In
fact, a confluence of forces led to the rapid decline of a
continued prevalent Irish presence in Holt County,
Nebraska. One aspect was the highly publicized misfortune
of an Irish colonization project in Graceville, Minnesota, in
1880, which called into question the feasibility of placing
indigent Irish immigrants directly on the land. The
Graceville settlers returned to urban environs after one
harsh winter on the prairie, and their misfortunes led to
national and international misgivings about such projects.

19. Noonan, p. 27.
20. "Saint Patrick's Parish O'Neill, Nebraska 125 Years," (O'Neill: St. Patrick's Church,
2002). Aric Pearson discovered the published parish history during his fieldwork.
21. Henthorne, p. 138.

The Minnesota colonization catastrophe led Bishop O'Connor of Omaha to refuse to accept such "unprepared" emigrants in his Nebraska settlements.[22] As promoters and bankers began to lose confidence in the prospects for naive Irish immigrants to become farmers, coupled with the absence of O'Neill's zealous efforts to bring more Irish to the community, other white European and Protestant ethnic groups—particularly Germans and Scandinavians—began gradually to colonize the economically marginal agrarian region in Nebraska that the Irish had first settled. By 1891, both non-Irish Presbyterian and Methodist populations had churches of their own in O'Neill.[23]

From its inception, the community of O'Neill was imagined by its founders and others as an Irish Catholic colonization project, based upon a collective notion of Irishness invoked in the named peoplehood of "the Irish" and their shared experience as destitute immigrants. The town's Irish identity was further instantiated in the political project of General John O'Neill—one that was both transnationally epitomized in his Fenian invasions of Canada and locally commemorated in the contemporary community as "authentically" Irish. In the beginning years of the European-American colonization of O'Neill, Irish Catholics formed the nucleus of the town. In time, the visible presence of a named Irish community shifted as other white European immigrants continued to populate the town into the early years of the twentieth century.

22. On planned settlements, see: James P. Shannon, *Catholic Colonization on the Western Frontier* (New Haven: Yale University Press, 1957); Malcolm Campbell, "Immigrants on the Land: Irish Rural Settlements in Minnesota and New South Wales, 1880–1910," *New Hibernia Review*, 2,1 (Spring, 1998), 43–61. On the Graceville settlement, see Bridget Connelly, *Forgetting Ireland: Uncovering a Family's Secret History* (St. Paul: Borealis Books, 2003). Connelly argues that the Graceville settlers have been unfairly characterized as unready, and were in fact victimized by Bishop John Ireland and other developers.
23. Henthorne, *The Irish Catholic Colonization Association of the United States*, p. 138.

It was fewer than one hundred years later that the citizens of O'Neill, Nebraska, rediscovered their Irishness in the mid-1960s through celebrations, public displays, and local parades. The town's nationalist founder had explicitly ridiculed those Irish who would forget their collective struggle, and had chastised those who would express their collective identity by merely "marching up Broadway in New York or any other city in the United States on St. Patrick's Day."[24] Ironically, such parading was precisely the manner in which the descendants of his community sought to commemorate his legacy. In 1967, approximately 3,500 residents of O'Neill initiated a local annual celebration of St. Patrick's Day, complete with Irish folk dance performances, a formal parade, the presence of governmental officials, and "authentic" O'Neills like my grandmother to represent the town's heritage. Both the broader history of national social movements in the United States, and the particular innovation of local entrepreneurship in the community, made it possible for the townspeople to recollect and perform Irishness in this way.

In United States, the period of the mid-1960s was marked by pressing questions of ethnic and national identity, fueled by the Civil Rights movement and black nationalism. Many black leaders and others involved in civil rights struggles questioned the inferior position of African Americans within the American nation, and fought against a racism based upon perceptions of inherent difference that persisted despite advances in legal equality. Challenging the hegemonic notion of cultural assimilation as a prerequisite to becoming fully and successfully "American," blacks

24. John O'Neill, "Public Address," p. 10.

mobilized around notions of social difference erected upon unique historical traditions and collective cultural practices. Such an emphasis on, and valorization of, cultural distinctiveness spurred a concomitant ethnic revival among white European groups in the United States during the latter half of the 1960s.[25] Public attention to ethnic customs and traditions in the form of celebrations like Kwanzaa and Columbus Day inaugurated a plethora of new, distinctively ethnic parades and festivals throughout the country. Ethnicity–which had previously been an identity to overcome in pursuit of American national homogenization–came to re-emerge in a new way "such that it provided ethnic identification with a positive status that few would have thought possible a decade earlier."[26] Thus, when the citizens of O'Neill, Nebraska, poured into the streets on St. Patrick's Day in 1967, they were not only reinventing and revalorizing Irishness, but also participating in a national trend that highlighted the social significance of ethnic identity for many Americans.

But, because ethnicity was newly valued in the United States, it was also potentially profitable–a possibility that the citizens of O'Neill came to explore fully. One of the few still-living citizens who remembered the pre-1967 St. Patrick's Day festivities spoke critically of local Irish-American celebrations that involved solely carnivalesque behavior, like painting a local Irish farmer's white horse green and marching it through the pubs. In other words, earlier "Irish" activities were remembered as particular family-specific practices that were usually playful and potentially disorderly, without any necessary communal benefit for the town. *The Holt County Independent* conveyed this perspective:

25. David Colburn and George Pozzetta, "Race, Ethnicity, and the Evolution of Political Legitimacy," in *The Sixties: From Memory to History,* ed David Farber, pp. 119–48. (Chapel Hill: University of North Carolina Press, 1994).
26. Colburn and Pozzetta, p. 139.

Some of the local Irishmen decided that St. Patrick's Day was not celebrated like it used to be, so they decided to have a parade all of their own. In the parade were Joe Cavanaugh, Joe Langan, Peter Mathews, Gene Mathews, and Jim Mathews. The first thing done was to buy up all the green food coloring in town and then procede [sic] to dye a white horse green. After this was accomplished, a car was decked out in green and the parade was underway. We understand they tried first to put two saddles on "Old Greeny" but decided that it might not be the best thing, so one came off.[27]

This was not the tenor of the ethnic event that 1967's official organizers had in mind. In line with new conceptions of ethnicity, the Jaycees, and, soon after, the local Chamber of Commerce, initiated tamer, and more commercial, activities to commemorate the saint's day. They also self-consciously framed these activities as tourist attractions designed to bring visitors and capital into the town. A weekend was devoted to the celebration that centered around a parade, which culminated with the town's children performing "Irish" dances on the "world's largest shamrock" strategically painted on the street at the intersection of two major highways closed for the event. The ethnic performance was the brainchild of a local entrepreneur, Vivian Melena, transplanted to the prairie from New York. As recounted by local residents, Mrs. Melena founded the dance troupe during 1967 in anticipation of the grand event. She used her training as a choreographer and experience with American folk dances to create routines to be performed by the local youth in the spirit of

---

27. "Green Horse Helps Irish to Celebrate St. Patrick's Day Friday," *Holt County Independent*, 23 March 1961.

ethnic heritage as well as to bolster her own dance studio business in town—a business that remains viable in twenty-first century O'Neill.

The entrepreneurial commercialization of Irish ethnic identity by citizens of O'Neill is evident in the narrative told by another descendant of the eponymous general, William O'Neill, who spent his childhood and early adult years on a family farm in rural Nebraska. He and his wife moved to O'Neill for the business potential related to marketing Irish culture in a gift shop that they envisioned in the town. He explained,

> We came up here, me and my wife Pat, probably fifteen years ago, fourteen years ago, for Saint Patrick's . . . So we saw up here in O'Neill a town that was with a lot of . . . third and fourth generation Irish who wanted to be very Irish, but there was nothing . . . they didn't know the direction to go in . . . . There's people who wanted a connection to Ireland, to their Irishness, and to their Irish heritage, and there was no path for them to that connection . . . . my last name being O'Neill, I thought William O'Neill from O'Neill, Nebraska, would help me in shopping and being on the internet.[28]

Their shop, Saints and Shillelaghs, has indeed been successful and remains highly visible in the local cultural imaginary of the town.

This self-conscious intent to marry ethnic heritage with tourism materialized in Governor Norbert T. Tiemann's official proclamation on St. Patrick's Day in 1969. The governor justified the recognition of O'Neill, Nebraska, as

---

28. William O'Neill, interview with Ilana Meltzer, March 20, 2005, O'Neill, Nebraska, in the Shamrocks and Shillelaghs store.

the state's "Irish Capital" thus: "Citizens of O'Neill have displayed their ability to translate their existing resources and talents into a tourist attraction."[29] Pat Fritz, the current director of the Chamber of Commerce and parade organizer for the past twenty-four years, focused on the economic importance of the St. Patrick's Day festivities for the local community:

> It is extremely important to restaurants, filling stations, and motels and bars. . . . Every single thing that brings people to our community is important, economically. Every out of town dollar is one that the local people aren't sharing.[30]

As Irish ethnic identity became culturally and economically valuable, its links to notions of collectivity were reconfigured. The Irish identity of the original settlers was firmly rooted in collective struggles in a perceived exile; later notions of Irish ethnicity came to be erected upon individual experiences. As the anthropologist Reginald Byron points out, for most European Americans,

> The everyday lived experience that once went with being ethnic has largely disappeared, allowing individuals the latitude to decide when, how, and in what degree—if at all—to express their attachment to their ancestry. . . . Identity with one's ancestral origins becomes optional, a matter of personal inclination and interpretation.[31]

Interestingly, the emphasis upon the individual as the locus of ethnic identity among European Americans is, in turn,

29. Norbert T. Tiemann, "Proclamation" (Nebraska State Historical Society, 1969), p. 1.
30. Pat Fritz, interview with D. Douglas Caulkins, March 20, 2005, Chamber of Commerce offices.
31. Reginald Byron, *Irish America* (Oxford: Oxford University Press, 1999), p. vi.

underwritten by American notions of national identity.[32] As Bonnie Urciuoli, an ethnographer who writes on Hispanic Americans, remarks, "The idea of an ethnic community is strongly infused with an American notion of individualism."[33] American national identity is firmly anchored in the notion of the individual who is a "self-motivated agent" that is upwardly mobile and hard working.[34] This specific individuation of ethnicity emerged as a particularly–though not exclusively–American phenomenon after the black Civil Rights movement, at which time ethnicity became a valued personal trait that allowed one to be a member of a distinct ethnic group as well as a "good" American.[35] In this manner, Irish ethnic identity in rural Midwest America became tantamount to what an individual has, does, and feels.

It is this conceptualization of Irishness–an individual enactment and interpretation, rather than a collectively shared and lived experience–that my grandmother's seven daughters and one son passed down to their children. While she was alive, the daughters of Mary O'Neill would recognize the importance St. Patrick's Day had for their mother and would send cards and make phone calls that included such ceremonial utterances as, "This is your day, Black Irish." The strong tie to an Irish identity that Mary O'Neill's children attributed to her was not something they necessarily recognized as important in their own daily lives. One of them recently reminded me, "When we have a drink on St. Patrick's Day we do it, in a sense, to remember her."

32. See: Herve Varenne, "Collective Representation in American Anthropological Conversations about Culture: Culture and the Individual," *Current Anthropology*, 25,3 (1984), 281–99; Bonnie Urciuoli, *Exposing Prejudice: Puerto Rican Experiences of Language, Race, and Class* (Boulder: Westview Press, 1996).

33. Urciuoli,p. 30.

34. Varenne, p. 281.

35. For a discussion of a similar phenomenon in another culture, see Fredrick Errington and Deborah Gewertz. "The Individuation of Tradition in a Papua New Guinean Modernity," *American Anthropologist*, 91,1 (1996), 114–26.

In my family, as in many Midwestern Irish-American ones, the importance of Irish ethnicity presumes that the previous generation had assigned it a significance that eludes their own time today—that is to say, the ethnicity being observed bears little connection to the present and no connection to collective histories outside the family.

William O'Neill, the owner of the local import store, who recognizes the elusive nature of Irishness for many of his customers, articulated efforts to realize a sense of identity in both individual and elective ways:

> For some Irish, for some people, there's truly a connection to the island, to the country—deeper than you can describe . . . when they go back it's like they've made that connection, back to the earth, back to the island, back to something there and they experience that almost like a religious experience . . . it's the subtleness of it, and the deeper meaning, and they really do have a connection . . . you can have five children in a family, and maybe two or three feel that, or express that, or want to show their Irishness like that, feel that, and the others don't. Maybe it's possible the mother or father does and the others don't. But I can definitely see people who come into the shop who, have that connection to Ireland, who feel that, and it's almost like a, a personal bond with them. I have that connection, and I feel that way.[36]

As O'Neill expresses it, the quest in time and space for an understanding of Irish identity manifests itself intermittently among the descendants of Irish immigrants. Traversing selectively among people like a spark, Irishness becomes

36. O'Neill interview, March 20, 2005.

discernible in those who carry what he terms "Celtic traits." Still, even among those who possess a connection, individual social actors must decide whether or not they wish to act upon their affective desire—to "show their Irishness." From this perspective, experiences of Irishness are expressions of particular embodied sentiments felt by the individual "I," as in "I have that connection, and "I feel that way," rather than the plural "we" of an ethnic community, as in "we are bound in this manner."

The individuation of ethnicity manifests itself further in public displays of Irishness—instantiated, among other ways, in my grandmother's delight in my red hair, or her insistence that dresses for parades must be green. It is also manifested in O'Neill where locals underscore the public and enacted aspects of their ethnic identity in their reflections on "being Irish." For instance, Noreen Cavanaugh Vega reminisced about the significance of her Irish identity during her childhood only a few decades ago:

> I danced with the O'Neill Irish Dancers on that very shamrock when I was in high school and drank many a green beer in the several "Irish" pubs in town when I was in college. My sisters and I were able to recite the Irish Blessing by heart and dance a jig well before junior high. And, to hear my dad, in his beautiful tenor voice, sing "Danny Boy" could quiet a rowdy St. Patrick's Day bar crowd and bring tears to your eyes.[37]

As recounted here, the individuation of ethnicity carries with it the potential of making an entrance into the larger space of community and the more affective domain

---

37. Noreen Cavanaugh Vega, "Commentary: Being Irish, It's More Than Wearing Green," March 23, 2000, www.dcmilitary.com/army/standard/archives/mar23/fd_b32300.html

of collectivity. However, individually gratifying and com-
mercially successful public performances—singing, dancing, reciting, and drinking—momentarily resolve the tension between individualism and collectivity by conveying
a sense that one's individuality is enhanced, rather than
diminished, by ethnic life ways.[38] This conception of Irish
identity—based upon the choice of individual participation
and enactment, rather than on the necessity of collective
shared histories and commitments—was the conception
that became active in the cultural imaginary of Irish Americans in O'Neill when they inaugurated their official local
civic celebrations of St. Patrick's Day.

Individual performances and enactments of Irishness
are clearly meaningful for, and display the ethnic identity
of, persons of Irish descent in O'Neill, Nebraska. Addition-
ally, the public spaces convey the symbolic presence and
importance of the town's Irish heritage. Signs of Irishness
abound along the highway from beginning to end. Upon
entering, one is greeted by a green and white sign pro-
claiming: "Welcome to O'Neill: Irish Capital of Nebraska."
At the opposite end of town, the image of local children
dancing Irish gigs on the Nebraska prairie covers an exterior wall of the Dan Ryan Theater for all passerbys to
appreciate. In between, shamrocks blanket everything
from real estate offices to hardware stores. It is a well-exe-
cuted spectacle for visitors, but also quite moving to travel-
ers of Irish descent. I admit that I was delighted by an
array of such public images that greeted me when I arrived
in O'Neill during October, 2004, to revisit the site of my

38. See Fredrick Errington, "Reflexivity Deflected: The Festival of Nations as an American
Cultural Performance," *American Ethnologist*, 14, 4 (1987), 654–67.

grandmother's parade and learn more of her experiences in the community from an ethnographic perspective.

I was working alongside my senior colleague, Doug Caulkins, who is a student of Welsh diaspora populations. Our investigation into Irish identity began by visiting local establishments and institutions where we assumed—incorrectly, as it turned out—that we would find locals who identified themselves as Irish or Irish-American. Our first stop was the Blarney Stone, a restaurant that proudly serves large steaks of corn-fed Nebraska cattle, deep-fried shrimp, and the usual array of cheese sticks, nachos, and onion rings one finds in Midwestern family restaurants. During our meal, we casually queried the waitress about Irish food on the menu. She politely smiled and pointed us to the potato skins. Certain that the Blarney Stone would indeed have some discernable connection to Irish culture or heritage, I asked the friendly young cashier while paying our bill about the proprietors of the establishment: "Are they Irish?" A bit confused by the odd question, the cashier was kind enough to inform us that the owners of the Blarney Stone were not Irish, but they were definitely Catholic. The vast majority of local people with whom we spoke— historians, librarians, and business people—did not identify as Irish or Irish-American. Further, they had a hard time identifying any Irish Americans in the community other than the gift store's William O'Neill.

I insisted that we attend Mass at St. Patrick's Church; surely we would find some clear evidence of Irish history and culture in the town's oldest parish. However, even on the St. Patrick's Day Mass in March, 2005, during the height of the community's celebration, there was not a word uttered before, during, or after the service that had anything to do with St. Patrick, nor any discourse remotely informed by Irish history or tradition. In short, we struggled to find the "Irish" in the Irish capital of Nebraska.

The demographic data supports our ethnographic data, showing a scarcity of Irish-identified population in O'Neill during the final decades of the twentieth century.[39] The census also contextualized our ethnographic evidence by showing this small population to be dwindling. In 1980, Holt County had an entire population of 13,552 people, of which the largest concentration was in the county seat, O'Neill. Of those, only 1,151 claimed Irish as their primary ancestry. An additional 1,773 people claimed Irish ancestry in conjunction with another ethnic group.[40] Thus, a total of 2,924 people—only 21.6 percent of the area's population—had some form of identification with Irish ethnicity. Declining trends continued in 1990 when, of a total population of 12,599 in the county, only 1,422 claimed Irish as their first ancestry, while an additional 1,014 claimed Irish as one of two ethnicities.[41] Thus, 2,436 individuals, or a mere 19.3 percent of people in the county, self-identified as possessing some Irish ancestry. As the general population in the area declined, so did the small numbers of Irish-identified people. A decade later, there were 11,551 people in Holt County, of which 1,079 listed Irish as their primary ancestry and an additional 979 listed it as their second, for a total of 2,058 people who self-identified as Irish.[42] At the beginning of the twenty-first century, only 17.81 percent of the county's population claimed to understand themselves as Irish in some way.

39. "The 1980 census marked the first time that a general question on ancestry (ethnicity) was asked in a decennial census. The question was based on self-identification and was open ended." United States Bureau of the Census, Population Division, 1980 Census of Population, "Definitions and Explanation of Subject Characteristics for the Census" (United States Department of Commerce, 1983), p. B8.

40. United States Bureau of the Census, Population Division, 1980 Census of Population. Volume 1: Characteristics of the Population, Part 29, Nebraska (United States Department of Commerce, 1983), p. 33–34.

41. http://factfinder.census.gov

42. http://factfinder.census.gov

The paradox of a celebrated Irish capital with so few self-identified Irish citizens was first explained to us by a no-nonsense elderly woman who owned a bustling coffee shop on the main street: "We're all Irish. Anyone can be Irish, really." Similar sentiments were echoed repeatedly during the course of our research. The citizens of O'Neill perceived no disjuncture between the facts of collective history, the displays of their ongoing public performances of Irish ethnicity, and the paucity of an Irish-American population in town. Noreen Cavanaugh Vega clearly negated the necessity of Irish heritage when she wrote, "The town today is less Irish by heritage, but Irish just the same."[43]

The ideology that "anyone can be Irish" was unabashedly promoted by the Nebraska legislature in its official proclamation of 1978, a document that provided an institutional endorsement of O'Neill's claims to be the "Irish Capital of Nebraska":

> Whereas the city of O'Neill, Nebraska has for time immemorial been known as the Irish capital of Nebraska and in fact the Irish capital of the nation and, at least in the opinion of some, the Irish capital of the world; and Whereas, on St. Patrick's day each year, all who set foot in the city of O'Neill become, if they desire, honorary Irishmen for at least a while.[44]

Thus, the discourse of official institutions, and of local individuals, effectively erases history in such a way that identity becomes a willed object, a mere desire to be fulfilled. The elective nature of Irish ethnicity for the descendants of Irish immigrants has been extended to an elective

43. Cavanaugh Vega, "Commentary: Being Irish," p. 1.
44. Legislative Resolution 186 Legislative Journal of the State of Nebraska, Volume 3 (Nebraska State Historical Society, 1978), p. 1297.

option for all European Americans. This marks the third, and current, conception of Irishness in O'Neill, Nebraska.

Irish identity began as an identity based upon collective experiences of migration to a new land and economic hardship among the early colonists of O'Neill. Their experiences as immigrants in search of a new home, coupled with General O'Neill's devoted nationalism, solidified a common sense of Irishness among the town's founding citizens. In time, this conception of identity shifted away from the group and toward individual experiences of ethnicity, manifested in performances and public displays that began during the national resurgence of European-American ethnicity that followed prominent Civil Rights movement of black Americans in the 1960s. Simultaneously commodified and individualized, Irish ethnicity gradually became an option, a matter of individual preference, a choice based upon personal style.

Such an understanding of Irish-American ethnic identity enabled the conceptual extension of Irishness for all Americans who wanted to make such a claim. Shaping the town's celebratory festivities on St. Patrick's Day, this conceptual extension of Irishness avails itself to O'Neill, as to other American towns. Byron's comments on the festivities of St. Patrick's Day in Albany, New York, could just as well been made about the celebrations on the Midwestern prairie: "as a celebration of unethnic Americanness: to be 'Irish' on St. Patrick's Day is to claim membership of the fully assimilated mainstream of middle Americans who have left the cultural baggage of their immigrant origins behind them."[45]

In political and economic terms, ethnicity for white Americans in O'Neill, Nebraska does not constitute the

45. Byron, p. 16.

same meaningful category of social difference it once did.[46] Going beyond Byron's explanation, I suggest it is this precisely the depoliticization of ethnic identity that allows for all European ethnicities of white Americans to be perceived as equal, and therefore interchangeable. In promoting public performances and celebratory invocations of ethnic identity, communities may also sidestep the complex issues that they face. Errington's ethnographic research on such festivals in Montana demonstrates that "by attributing contemporary importance to what has actually become a socially irrelevant issue [ethnicity], people present a significantly distorted view of both past and present."[47] The uncritical perpetuation of Irish identity in O'Neill may well serve to obfuscate issues of inequality and marginalization that are also part of the social fabric of twenty-first-century Midwest America.

The governor's proclamation mentioned earlier specifically lauds the interchangeability of white ethnic groups' identities. While recognizing the Nebraska Irish, it simultaneously pays equal tribute to the heritage of other white European settlers: "The Nebraska Irish . . . with the Czech, Swedish, German, English, and Danish, and other nationalities—helped to make Nebraska this great proud and bountiful state."[48] In this way, the ahistorical claim that "We're all Irish" can be regarded as a discourse constitutive of American national identity—albeit in locally instantiated forms.

---

46. Caulkins has analyzed this transition in O'Neill as a movement from ethnicity-based bonding social capital to a locality-based social capital. The latter allows every resident to be Irish regardless of ethnic heritage. Douglas Caulkins, "From Ethnicity Celebration to Community Festival: Phases of Formalization of Social Capital," paper presented at "Reassessing Civil Society, the State, and Social Capital: Theory, Evidence, Policy," University of Bergen Centre for Development Studies, Hardanger, Norway, May 11–13, 2006.
47. Errington, 658.
48. Norbert T. Tiemann, *Proclamation, March 17, 1969* (Nebraska State Historical Society, 1969).

James E. Doan

∾

How the Irish and Scots Became Indians: Colonial Traders and Agents and the Southeastern Tribes

In recent years such books as Noel Ignatiev's *How the Irish Became White* have challenged assumptions about Irish identity in America, and essays in such collections as Bayor and Meagher's *The New York Irish* have illustrated the rich cultural fusions of the Irish with African Americans and Asians in nineteenth-century New York. The question of how the Irish interacted and melded with non-white groups interests me on both a personal and a professional level. I first came to this topic as a result of my interest in the background of my own grandmother, Gladys Burke, whom I knew to be of Irish and Native American descent. I found that this genetic combination was actually fairly common among people I met, generally Southerners of Irish or Scotch-Irish and Indian descent whose ancestors came to America during the eighteenth century. The usual oral history is of an Indian "princess" marrying a white man, typically a trader, agent, or fur trapper. My research also showed that the women were frequently prominent in their tribes, with the husband gaining status through the marriage, and their children inheriting the best of both cultural, linguistic, and socioeconomic worlds, at least until the white expansion of the early nineteenth century.

With this essay, I hope to spark further debate on the relations between early Irish and Scots immigrants to America and the native population.

———

Scots and Irish traders and agents, who often wrote about their experiences, were prominent among the Europeans who settled among the southeastern Indians in the eighteenth century—particularly among the Cherokees, Choctaws, Chickasaws, Creeks, and Seminoles, collectively known as the Five Civilized Nations. One such trader was the Scotsman James Adair, author of *History of the American Indians* (1755), who knew Greek, Latin, Hebrew, Spanish, French, and Irish, in addition to the Indian languages needed in his work. Adair came to South Carolina about 1730 and lived among the Cherokees and Muskogee Creeks for forty years, dying soon after the outbreak of the American Revolution. After completing a study of the southeastern Indians' customs and rituals, Adair advanced the theory that the Native Americans were actually one of the ten lost tribes of Israel.

Adair did not have a high opinion of the ordinary packhorsemen, traders, and hirelings who drifted through the Indian country, whom he called "mean reprobate pedlars," though he did have some respect for the "regular traders" who showed more stability. Other observers echoed his disdain for the early traders. "The Traders from Georgia," one eighteenth-century observer wrote, were "a monstrous set of Rogues for the major Part of whom the Gallows groans," and Caleb Swan vilified them as "the most abandoned wretches than can be found, perhaps, on this side of Botany Bay."[1]

1. Cited in J.W. Martin, *Sacred Revolt: The Muskogees' Struggle for a New World* (Boston: Beacon Press, 1991), p. 78.

John Rea from Ballynahinch, County Down, was one of the earliest settlers in Georgia after the colony was founded in 1733. He became an Indian trader and a partner of Irishman Patrick Brown, George Galphin from County Armagh, and the Scotsman Lachlan McGillivray. Originally based on the Savannah River near Augusta, in 1765 they obtained a grant of 50,000 acres on which to settle Irish immigrants, in a settlement called Queensborough, near present-day Louisville, Georgia.[2] In time they expanded their operations to Pensacola, Mobile, and elsewhere in the new colonies of West and East Florida, which the British acquired from the French and Spanish, respectively, according to the 1763 Treaty of Paris.

After the French and Spanish departed from the southeast, trade with the Indians fell primarily into the hands of Galphin and his partners. Headquartered at Silver Bluff, near the South Carolina and Georgia border, Galphin's firm "possessed the most extensive trade, connections and influence among the South[ern] Indian tribes, particularly with the Muskogees [Creeks] and Chactaws." European goods included blankets, hardware, cooking utensils, ornaments, and rum, for which the Indians traded corn, slaves captured from other tribes – a practice that continued at least until the 1730s – and, increasingly, furs and skins, particularly from the white-tailed deer. Galphin's ruthless and exploitative traders routinely used devious means to cheat the Indians, the most common strategy involving alcohol. Adair wrote:

Many Traders . . . have made a constant Practice of [carrying] very little Goods, but chiefly, and for the most part intierly Rum from Augusta, from whence

2. E.R.R. Green, "The Irish in American Business and Professions," in *America and Ireland, 1776–1976: The American Identity and the Irish Connection*, ed. D. N. Doyle and O. D. Edwards (Westport: Greenwood Press, 1980), p. 197.

as soon as the Indian Hunters are expected in from
their Hunts, they set out with small or large Quanti-
tites of that bewitching Liquor according to their
Ability. Then some of the Rum Traders place themselves near the Towns, in the way of the Hunters
returning home with their deer Skins. The poor
Indians . . . are unable to resist the Bait; and when
Drunk are easily cheated.[3]

In his report on the trade, Emund Atkin related how
the hunters found themselves stripped of "the fruit of three
or four Month Toil . . . without the means of buying the
necessary Clothing for themselves or their Families . . .
Their Domestick and inward Quiet being broke, Reflection sours them, and disposes them for Mischief."[4]

Such areas as Silver Bluff became centers of a multira-
cial, multicultural society. Located on the Savannah
River and just below the major trading path from South
Carolina to the Lower Muskogees, Silver Bluff was ani-
mated with the comings and goings of Creek hunters, as
well as Irish, Scots, and English traders, African and
African-American slaves, cowboys, and packhorsemen,
British colonial officials, land speculators, and frontier
farm families. It was a borderland area where the three
races freely intermingled. Polygamy had been a common
practice among the Creek political, religious, and economic elite and the traders who dealt closely with them—
who achieved considerable status in Creek society—often
had several wives and mistresses. For example, George
Galphin's will, probated in 1782, reveals that he had two
children by a *métis*[5] woman named Rachel Dupree, one

---

3. Adair, *History of the American Indians*, cited in Martin, p. 66.
4. Adair, cited in Martin, p. 66.
5. I prefer the French term "*métis*" to the English "half-breeds." In French, the term means
"mixed-bloods," is less pejorative than the English term, and is semantically equivalent to
Spanish *mestizos*.

by an Indian named Nitshukey, and three by two black women called Sappho and Mina. In addition, Galphin had earlier married Catherine Saunderson in Ulster, and a Bridget Shaw in Charleston, South Carolina.[6]

The southeastern tribes were matrilineal and matrilocal, and so marriage to outsiders of a different ethnic group—including escaped African-American slaves—did not constitute a problem, as any offspring would be considered members of their mother's clan. We find considerable intermarriage between Indian women and European traders from the late seventeenth century onward. Among the Muskogee Creeks, for example, there were two types of marriage. One was a fairly casual, profane version called "a make haste marrriage." Arranged between a male visitor and a female of the tribe, such a liaison entailed few obligations and could be terminated by either party; most of the relations between Indian women and European traders were probably of this kind. However, the Muskogees and others also practiced a more permanent marital bond, which was embraced by a minority of traders. When men and women married seriously, it was a sacred event, with a whole sequence of symbolic and material actions, including the exchange of gifts. Throughout the southeast, the European traders who married and settled with native women became assimilated into the village or town where they lived. Unlike native men, however, who would go on long hunts in the fall and winter, the Europeans tended to stay in one place, perhaps tending to a small farm or some stock of pigs, horses, and cattle. As their holdings became larger, they became more attached to the village where their property was located. Known as "Indian countrymen" by the Anglo-Americans,

6. David C. Crass, et al., "A Man of Great Liberality: Recent Research at George Galphin's Silver Bluff" (South Carolina Institute of Archaeology and Anthropology, Columbia, 1997), p. 32.

these traders would learn the Indian laws and customs. Adair refers to them as "white people . . . who have become Indian proselytes of justice, by living according to the Indian religious system."[7] He notes, too, that the "Indian countrymen" were no longer Christian; these Irish and Scots traders had gone beyond their original orientations, abandoned patriarchal culture, and learned to live as Indians. Their children were to prove extremely important to the tribes in the coming generations.

The *métis* were part of two cultures, belonging entirely to neither. They were often unsure whether their father's surname or their mother's clan was more important. Some, such as the Creeks George Stiggins and Thomas Woodward, blended into white society. Even for those who remained among their fellow tribesmen, the pull of white society was strong. At the end of the nineteenth century, for example, the Creek Graysons of Oklahoma—descended from the British trader Robert Grierson—traced their ancestry through male Scottish ancestors rather than along matrilineal clan lines. One of the most acculturated *métis*, William McIntosh, was the son of a Coweta Creek of the Wind clan and Captain William McIntosh, a British agent to the Lower Creeks during the Revolution. The younger McIntosh amassed a fortune in land, slaves, and livestock. He ultimately identified with the group in favor of ceding Creek lands to the United States government and removal to an area west of the Mississippi; McIntosh was executed on orders of the Creek National Council in 1825.[8]

George Galphin's partner, Lachlan McGillivray, had taken as one of his wives a woman of mixed Creek and French descent, named Sehoy. Their son, Alexander

7. Adair, cited in Martin, p. 78.
8. J. L. Wright, *Creeks and Seminoles: Destruction and Regeneration of the Muscogulge People* (Lincoln: University of Nebraska Press, 1986), pp.166–67, 238–40.

McGillivray, is emblematic of the rise of the *métis* and their influence on Native American politics in the late eighteenth and nineteenth centuries. Born in Little Tallassee in what is now Alabama in 1759, he inherited political status from his mother's Wind Clan and economic power from his father. His father sent him to two of the best schools in Charleston and Savannah, but his education was cut off by the war. He then became an assistant to the Tory John Stuart, Scottish-born Superintendent of Southern Indian Affairs, and led the Upper Creeks in support of George III. As a chief, he sought and achieved British protection for the Creek nation and was appointed an honorary British colonel. During the war, his elderly father left for the Scottish Highlands and turned over his commercial interests to his nephew, John McGillivray, in Pensacola.

When the Revolutionary War ended in 1783, the Creeks discovered that their lands now lay within the borders of the new United States. Having been previously concerned with promoting trade and commerce with whites, the Creeks were suddenly forced to change their policy vis-à-vis non-Indians; they now needed to concern themselves with defending their tribal boundaries and with preserving their independence against the United States. During the war a number of Scottish traders, including William Panton, John Leslie, Thomas Forbes, William Alexander, and Charles McLatchy, had fled to East Florida, where they continued to trade with the Creeks and Seminoles. After 1783, they asked the Spanish government to let them remain in the province and continue this commerce. Although the Spanish distrusted these Scottish Tories, the alternatives were worse: arrangements with the French had failed and the impatient Indians needed supplies. Reluctantly, Spanish authorities allowed Panton,

Leslie, and company to remain in East Florida, then to build a warehouse in Apalachee on the Wakulla River and, in time, outposts at Pensacola, Mobile, and elsewhere.

Panton moved to Pensacola from St. Augustine in 1784 to resume trade with the Indians. Gradually, his company expanded its operations from St. Augustine to the Mississippi River. In time Spain granted the company a virtual monopoly of the Indian trade throughout the entire southeast. Panton's silent partner, McGillivray, served as a powerful middleman in both the deerskin trade and in imperial politics. Both the company and the Spanish government—which had regained control of Florida from the British—supported his authority with gifts and a regular supply of goods, giving him great economic and political influence. Realizing the importance of establishing a united Creek nation, McGillivray attempted to buy time by negotiating treaties with both the United States and Spanish, thus adapting the Creeks' time-honored strategy of playing one side off against the other.

In 1784, McGillivray signed the Treaty of Pensacola with the Spanish, which recognized the independence of the Creek Nation and agreed to furnish them with guns, powder, and other necessities. The Spanish colonial government also appointed him its agent among the Creeks. In return, the Creek Nation promised to act as a buffer between the United States and Florida, and to keep Georgians out of Spanish territory. Armed with Spanish weapons, McGillivray sent Creek armies east and north to drive Georgia and Tennessee settlers from the Creek Nation. Not all Creeks supported a centralized government, fearing that individual Creek towns would lose their right to form their own policies. An opposing faction, led by chiefs Eneah Miko of Cusseta and Hopoithle Miko of the Tallassee town of Chattacchufaulee, also sought trade with the American citizens of Georgia and signed three treaties with the Georgia state government during the 1780s. McGillivray denounced the treaties as unauthorized and illegal, and gained much popular support as the documents signed by the breakaway group called for cession of a large area of Creek land. McGillivray, in effect, achieved a revolution in Creek politics "by placing the warriors in all cases over the micos or kings."[9]

When the Georgians killed some Lower Muskogee men in retaliation for crimes committed by the Upper Muskogees in 1787, the two factions "buried the hatchet," uniting under the "great chief" –McGillivray. In 1790, McGillivray led a delegation of Creek leaders to New York–the American capital at the time–to sign a treaty with George Washington. We have a description of him from this time by Abigail Adams, the vice-president's wife, who wrote that "he dresses in our own fashion, speaks English like a native . . . is not very dark, [and is] much of a gentleman."[10] Under the 1790 treaty, the United States recognized the sovereignty of the Creek Nation, acknowledged that the land cessions were illegal, approved McGillivray's plan for improving trade relations, and promised to protect the boundaries of the Creek Nation from encroachment by American citizens. In return, the Creeks sold the United States a three-million acre block of land for Georgia. According to a secret codicil, McGillivray was made a brigadier general in the American army, which would allow him access to top-level decision making.

Unfortunately for the Creeks, McGillivray died before his plans were completed. Plagued by illness for most of his life–his health was not helped by his well-known love of

9. Martin, p. 83.
10. Cited in Wright, p. 61.

whiskey—the chief died at Panton's home on February 17,
1793, at the age of 34. Befitting his role, his funeral was
attended by representatives of the three major powers with
which he had dwelt: Spain, Britain, and the United States.
Often considered the greatest of all Indian diplomats—a
later writer called him the "Talleyrand of Alabama"—The
Gentleman's Magazine of London printed an obituary hail-
ing McGillivray as a great statesman who, "with the vigour
of his mind, overcame the disadvantages of an education
had in the wilds of America."[11] The Georgians failed to
honor the terms of the 1790 treaty, and President Washington refused to force them to do so. Despite competition
from the United States government—which constructed a
"factory," actually a warehouse or trading center, at Col-
eraine on the St. Marys River near the border of Florida
and Georgia in the hope of taking over the Creek trade—
Panton, Leslie and Co., followed by Forbes and Co. after
1804, continued to dominate trade with the Creeks and
Seminoles until about 1820.[12] Meanwhile, the federal government launched a policy of trying to acculturate the
Creeks and other southeastern Indians into mainstream
American society. In 1796 Washington appointed Benjamin
Hawkins, a former congressman from North Carolina, as
the southeastern Indian superintendent, to oversee this pol-
icy, which lasted until the Creek War of 1813–15.

McGillivray's descendants continued to own large holdings near the Alabama River, until forced to cede them to
the Americans following the Creek War, which had been
instigated by a group of prophets or shamans, known as the
Red Sticks, seeking to ward off the impending destruction
of the Creek Nation. The Red Sticks included at least two
métis, Peter McQueen and Paddy Walsh, the latter

---

11. Cited in J. Hewitson, *Tam Blake & Co.: The Story of the Scots in America* (Edinburgh:
Canonate Press, 1993), p. 168.
12. Wright, p. 51.

recorded as a "great Indian linguist speaking the creek alabama chickasaw and choctaw languages fluently." Walsh was the adopted son of a Tory named James Walsh who had fled to Muskogee during the Revolution.[13] Paddy claimed to make men invincible to bullets—a claim that was all too sadly proven untrue, as more than 3,000 Creeks, about fifteen percent of the tribe's population, lost their lives during the war.[14]

The Florida Creek and Seminole leader Osceola, who fought against the United States army during the Second Seminole War of the 1830s, was also of mixed British, Irish, and Indian origin. Born Billy Powell, he was descended from a Scotsman, James McQueen, for whom early biographers give the astounding lifespan of 1683–1811! McQueen was the first white man to arrive in the Upper Creek town of Tallassee, near present-day Tuskegee, Alabama, sometime before 1716. There, he married a Tallassee woman and became prominent in Indian society. Their daughter, Nancy, married a man named Copinger, also probably of British or Irish descent; and Nancy's daughter, Polly, married the British trader William Powell in 1803, giving birth to Billy the next year. James McQueen's son Peter, head warrior of Tallassee and a prophetic leader or shaman during the Creek War, married Betsy, the daughter of Alexander McGillivray's sister Sophia and her mulatto husband, John Durant. By the time of Billy's birth, most of the community was of mixed British, Indian, and African blood.[15] A later joke reflects the racial diversity of the southeastern frontier:

a Creek said to a Cherokee . . . "You Cherokees are so mixed with whites we cannot tell you from

13. Martin, p. 126.
14. M. D. Green, *The Creeks* (New York: Chelsea House Press, 1990), p. 53.
15. Patricia Wickman, *Osceola's Legacy* (Tuscaloosa and London: University of Alabama Press, 1991), pp. xix–xx, 7–8.

whites." The Cherokee . . . replied: "You Creeks are
so mixed with Negroes we cannot tell you from
Negroes."[16]

The Cherokee chief during the "Trail of Tears" removal
to Oklahoma in 1838, who continued to lead his people
until after the Civil War, was Chief John Ross. He was
only one-eighth Cherokee by blood, an ancestry that
reflects the considerable intermarriage between Scots,
Irish, and Native Americans in the eighteenth and early
nineteenth century. The chief's maternal great-grandfather
was a Scotsman, William Shorey, who had served as an
interpreter for the British army during the French and
Indian Wars in the late 1750s. Shorey had married a
Cherokee woman, Ghigooie, a member of the Bird clan.
Ross's maternal grandfather, John McDonald, was born in
Inverness, Scotland, and came to Charleston in 1766 at the
age of nineteen. He pushed on to Savannah where he
worked for a mercantile establishment that carried on a
thriving trade with the southern Indians. He was sent by
his employers to Fort Loudon, in what is now Tennessee,
to trade with the Cherokees, marrying Ann Shorey, the
daughter of William and Ghigooie, and becoming an
active defender of Cherokee interests. Along with fellow
Scots John Stuart, the superintendent of southern Indian
affairs based in Mobile and later Pensacola, and Deputy
Commissioner of Indian Affairs Alexander Cameron, who
also married a Cherokee woman, McDonald understood
and argued for the Indian position when controversies
developed between traders and Cherokees.

The Cherokees were quite receptive to mixed white
and Indian marriages; the Cherokee chief Oconostota
wrote to John Stuart: "Mr. Cameron has got a son by a

16. Cited in Martin, p. 73.

Cherokee woman. We desire that he may educate the boy like the white people, and cause him to be able to read and write, that he may resemble both white and red, and live among us when his father is dead."[17] Much later, John and Ann McDonald's daughter, Molly, married the Scottish Daniel Ross and became the mother of Chief John Ross. During the American Revolution McDonald, who had settled near Ross's Landing in modern-day Chattanooga, was a Loyalist agent among the pro-British Chickamaugan Cherokees living in northwest Georgia and southern Tennessee. They were opposed to the Virginians who had begun settling in the Watauga River area, which led to some bitter fighting during the Revolution.

McDonald and Ross both tried to raise their families as Scots; young John reportedly begged his grandfather to allow him to wear the presumably more comfortable Indian clothes rather than Highland dress. Despite his upbringing, John Ross, whose Indian name was Cooweescoowee, remained Cherokee to the core. William McDonald has suggested that, "among the early migrants to America it was predominantly Scots who capitalized as influential men and leaders among the native Americans," which he attributes to "... their inherited background in the old Celtic clan system that gave them a natural advantage to assume leadership roles among the Indian tribes."[18]

During the 1760s and '70s, marriages of Cherokees and other southeastern Indians with Scots, English, Germans, and Irish became increasingly common. For example, Englishman Edward Graves married the Cherokee Lau-to-tau-yie and converted her to Christianity. Because she wished to please her husband by dressing herself and her

17. Cited in G. S. Woodward, *The Cherokees* (Norman: University of Oklahoma Press, 1963), p. 84.
18. Cited in Hewitson, p. 166.

children as whites, Graves made her a loom, sent to England for a spinning wheel, cards, and cotton, then taught her how to spin and weave cotton into cloth.[19]

In the late eighteenth century John Adair—born in 1758, and a descendant of a Limerick man, Robert Adair, who had married Arabella Campell of Galloway—married Ge-ho-ga Foster, a full-blood Cherokee of the Deer Clan. The modern Adair family of Sallisaw, Oklahoma, trace their ancestry to this marriage. Many of the Adairs were prominent, including Walter Adair, who was jailed along with other Cherokee chiefs in Georgia in 1835 for resisting the forced removal from their lands and died shortly thereafter. One of his sons became chief justice of the Cherokee Nation supreme court, and a grandson became a Cherokee judge. A great-great granddaughter, Mary Adair, an artist and teacher, and widow of the Pawnee Samuel Horse Chief, has stated, "Although we have been Cherokee Nation citizens for generations, we remember our Scots heritage."[20] George Lowrey married Nannie of the Holly Clan, and their son George, born about 1770, figured prominently in the affairs of the Cherokee nation until his death in 1852. Irishman Bryan Ward married Nancy, a member of the Wolf Clan, who was also a Ghigau or Beloved Woman, having won this honor when she was married to Kingfisher, whose place she took when he was killed in a battle with the Creeks.[21]

Proponents of Indian Removal during the 1820s and '30s found it useful to write and speak of the Indians as though the indigenous peoples of America were all nomadic hunters, underdeveloped children of the forest committed to a tribal way of life that was inferior to, and could not survive contact with, white civilization. It proved

19. Woodward, p. 85.
20. Hewitson, pp. 277–78.
21. Woodward, pp. 85–86.

quite embarrassing to American expansionists that the Indians most opposed to the removal were also the ones most fully assimilated to white culture. Cherokee John Ridge's 1826 "Essay on Cherokee Civilization" proudly proclaimed:

> the 14,000 citizens of "the Cherokee Nation" had their own National Council, a constitution, a court system, written laws, English newspapers and schools, farms with cattle and orchards, cotton plantations worked by 1,277 black slaves, and at least 200 interracial (red and white) married couples who owned private property.[22]

President Andrew Jackson—whose parents had left Carrickfergus, County Antrim, only months before his birth, and who is reported to have spoken with a broad Ulster accent—responded by appealing to the Constitution, claiming that the United States could not be a sovereign nation with secure rights if a separate nation were allowed to exist within its borders. But the legal arguments only reinforced the underlying cultural issue that had already been planted in the public's mind: the conviction that even the assimilated Indians could not adapt, but must be removed or face extinction.

In his autobiography, published anonymously in 1855, Sam Houston, also of Ulster Scots origin, stressed his frontier background, particularly his affinity for the Indians. In his teens, Houston left his family and white civilization to live as an adopted Cherokee, for "he prefered measuring deer tracks, to tape . . . he liked the wild liberty of the Red men, better than the tyranny of his own brothers . . .

---

22. Cited in *The Harper American Literature*, ed. Donald McQuade et al. (New York: Harper & Row, 1987), 1:730–31, cited in John McWilliams, *The Last of the Mohicans: Civil Savagery and Savage Civility* (New York: Twayne, 1995), p. 104.

runing wild among the Indians, sleeping on the ground, chasing wild game, living in the forest, and reading Homer's Iliad withal."[23] After a failed marriage had blighted his political career, he returned to the Cherokees, by then displaced to Oklahoma. Houston took as his second wife the Cherokee chief Ooleteka's niece, a widowed, mixed-blood Cherokee woman, Tiana Rogers Gentry. It was the custom of the future president of the Republic of Texas and hero of the Alamo to dress in full Indian regalia while in Washington as a tribal ambassador for the Cherokee nation in 1829.[24] When the call to Texas came he had been living for three years as the chief's adopted son.

Irish and Scottish links can be found with other southeastern tribes as well. The Loyalist trader James Colbert, a Scot who lived with the Chickasaws from his childhood, spoke Chickasaw fluently and had three Chickasaw wives. His half-dozen sons remained highly influential in Chickasaw councils well into the nineteenth century.[25] We find a similar pattern throughout the west, northwest, and Canada. According to Gary Nash,

> Irish trader John Johnson could not have done business in Indian villages without his Ojibway wife O-shaw-gus-co-day-wayquak, daughter of an Ojibway leader. Nor could Michael Lafranboise, a French immigrant, whose Okanogay wife paved the way for

23. Samuel Houston, "The Life of Sam Houston," pp. 22–24, cited in Richard Slotkin, *Regeneration through Violence: The Mythology of the American Frontier, 1600–1860* (Middletown: Wesleyan University Press, 1973), p. 429.

24. Gary B. Nash, "The Hidden History of Mestizo America," *The Journal of American History* 82, 3 (December, 1995), pp. 941–64.

25. Bernard Bailyn, "An American Tragedy," review of Colin G. Calloway, *The American Revolution in Indian Country: Crisis and Diversity in Native American Communities* in *New York Review of Books*, 5 October 1995, p. 14.

his trading with the Indians in Oregon Territory. Laframboise boasted about having a high-ranking wife in every Indian tribe inhabiting the region he worked as a trapper. The fabled Jim Bridger married three times, each time to an Indian woman, once to the daughter of Chieft Washakie of the Shoshone. Equally fabled Kit Carson had four wives: an Arapaho, a Cheyenne, a Mexican, and a Taos-born mestizo woman.[26]

The mestizo or *métis* population, bilingual and bicultural, functioned well in both Indian and Anglo-American societies. Because of the land greed of white Americans in the early nineteenth century, many of them were deported to the Indian Territory in what was to become the State of Oklahoma. However, many of their descendants–including myself–form a large part of the American population, and play an active role in preserving the traditions and memory of their European and Native American ancestors.

26. Nash, loc. cit.

LAWRENCE J. MCCAFFREY

∾

GOING MY WAY AND IRISH-AMERICAN CATHOLICISM: MYTH AND REALITY

My examinations of Irish-American history have always found that the experiences of assimilation and the breaking-down of barriers lie at the heart of the group's experience. As I wrote in the preface to *Textures of Irish America*, "I interpret the Irish journey in the United States from the unskilled working-class ghettos to the middle-class suburbs as a success story in acquisition of material prosperity if not necessarily a spiritual or intellectual achievement."[1] Without doubt, exclusion, hostility, and economic hardship have been a part of the Irish-American experience—often the part that makes the best story. But such estrangement was by no means the only, or even the most prominent, theme in the lives of Irish Americans in earlier days; theirs was also the story of a powerful drive toward financial security, respectability, and proof of their good citizenship.

Novels, plays, and sometimes the melodies and lyrics of popular songs can recall the atmosphere of past times more vividly than the efforts of historians. Films are especially effective. When teaching Irish-American history, I have often shown or assigned movies that illustrate the myths and realities of the subject, emphasizing that the former has often shaped the latter. These have included *A*

1. Lawrence McCaffrey, *Textures of Irish America* (Syracuse: Syracuse University Press, 1992), p. xi.

Long Day's Journey Into Night (1962), probably the best work of America's greatest playwright, Eugene O'Neill; *The Last Hurrah* (1958), a film version of Edwin O'Connor's famous political novel; *The Molly Maguires* (1970), a cinematic interpretation of Irish working-class unrest in the Pennsylvania coal fields; and two contrasting views of Irish-American Catholicism, the 1981 movie *True Confessions* and 1944's *Going My Way*.

In deciding on *Going My Way*, I wondered if a movie hit of the 1940s would appeal to present-day students. Their cultural, social, religious, and often suburban backgrounds radically differ from those of their urban, parish-focused Irish-American parents and grandparents. Unlike the old, new Catholic parishes have become multi-, rather than singly, ethnic and no longer are the heart and soul of a community. Few young Irish Americans enter religious life today, and those that do are seldom from the top talent layer of their ethnic group. Priests, nuns, and brothers no longer command the respect and obedience they claimed and enjoyed in pre-Vatican II days. Lately, pedophilia and other sexual scandals have further lowered the laity's esteem for males in religious life. Mass attendance, reception of the sacraments, and financial contributions to parishes have plummeted. Catholic insecurities and guilt feelings are more likely to be assuaged by Prozac or by psychological therapy than by a visit to the confessional on Saturday afternoons.

Paramount released *Going My Way* in May of 1944. It attracted large audiences and the following March won seven of nine Academy Awards, receiving Oscars for best picture, director (Leo McCarey), actor (Bing Crosby), supporting actor (Barry Fitzgerald), original story (McCarey), screenplay (Frank Butler and Frank Cavett), and song

(Johnny Burke's and Jimmy Van Heusen's "Swinging on a Star"). As we know from many recent examples, Academy Award winners are not necessarily the most excellent films of their year. In the music category, in a year when *Cover Girl* had Gene Kelly and Rita Hayworth singing and dancing to "Long Ago and Far Away," "Swinging on a Star" was not its equal–but I doubt if any other film surpassed the general quality of *Going My Way*. The New York Film Critics Circle Awards and the Golden Globe, USA, also gave best film and director titles to *Going My Way* and McCarey. Fitzgerald received further acknowledgement as best actor from the New York Film Critics and best supporting actor from Golden Globes, USA.

Going My Way was not the first time that Hollywood studios cast prominent actors as priests. In 1936, Spencer Tracy played Father Tim Mullin in *San Francisco*. His performance resulted in an Oscar nomination. Two years later, he won the Oscar as Father Edward Flanagan in *Boys' Town*. In 1941, Tracy reprised the same role in *Men of Boys' Town*. Pat O'Brien, who, like Tracy, was a Milwaukee Irish American, also wore a Roman collar on screen. In 1938, he portrayed Father Jerry Connolly in *Angels With Dirty Faces*. Two years later he played Father Francis Duffy, the courageous and uplifting chaplain in *The Fighting 69th*.

Although they concentrated on Irish-American priests, there were differences in the dominant themes of *San Francisco, Boy's Town, Men of Boys' Town, The Fighting 69th*, and *Going My Way*. Father Mullin, with the assistance of Mary Blake (Jeannete MacDonald), and the 1906 earthquake, persuaded his boyhood friend, "Blackie" Morton (Clark Gable) that a life of virtue was better than one of vice. Father Flanagan rescued boys from poverty, broken families, and various kinds of abuse and then educated them for productive lives. Father Connolly countered the corrupting example his old chum, gangster Rocky Sullivan (James Cagney), had on young men on the East Side of New York. Father Duffy tended to the spiritual needs and uplifted the morale of soldiers on the Western Front in World War I. *Going My Way* took place in a less dramatically charged setting; it was about a priest functioning in a parish, salvaging it from financial collapse while tending to the spiritual and secular problems of parishioners.[2]

For its time, *Going My Way* was a long film—126 minutes of humor, pathos, and song. It opens with Father Charles "Chuck" O'Malley (Bing Crosby) from East St. Louis, Illinois arriving at the rectory of St. Dominics's, a multi-ethnic but mostly Irish parish in Manhattan's East Side, to assist its Irish-born pastor, Father Fitzgibbon (Barry Fitzgerald). St. Dominic's is deeply in debt and banker Ted Haines Sr. (Gene Lockhart) is threatening to foreclose on the mortgage. Father Chuck negotiates with Haines, Sr., and later takes a group of delinquent teenage boys to a New York Yankee-St. Louis Browns baseball game and organizes them into a choir. He also offers financial and moral support to a runaway young woman, Carol James (Gene Heather). His guidance, expressed in the song "Going My Way," inspires a sense of responsibility in Carol, leading to her marriage with live-in boyfriend, Ted Haines, Jr. (James Brown), just before he enlists in the United States Army Air Force.

Despite his energy, charm, attractive appearance, and obvious dedication to his vocation, the crooning, gregarious, informal, nonchalant young Irish-American cleric irritates the kindhearted but gruff old pastor trained in

2. Terry Golway, "The Parish: The Building of Community," *The Irish in America*, ed. Michael Coffey and Terry Golway (New York: Hyperion, 1997), emphasizes *Going My Way* as a film about a Catholic urban parish.

the rigid, authoritarian ways of Irish Catholicism. When the singing of the boy's choir interrupts Fitzgibbon at prayers he finally decides to request O'Malley's transfer. But when he visits the bishop, the pastor discovers that his curate is a troubleshooter assigned specifically to rescue St. Dominic's from financial collapse. Unwilling to play second fiddle to his younger colleague, Fitzgibbon surreptitiously packs a bag and leaves the rectory. Returned rain-soaked by a lapsed Catholic Irish policeman (Tom Dillon), Fitzgibbon goes to bed with a slight cold. When a worried O'Malley comes to his room, they share a bit of the pastor's Irish whiskey, and Fitzgibbon mentions how much he misses his mother back in Ireland; the old priest's chronic money shortages, the result of his generosity to others, have prevented him from returning home for a visit. He asks the young priest to sing his favorite song, the one his mother used to sing when he was a young lad. O'Malley obliges with the lullaby "Too-Ra-Loo-Ra-Loo-Ral." From then on, they become close friends, O'Malley somewhat modernizing and softening the perspectives of Fitzgibbon. They even play golf with Father Chuck's high school friend and classmate, Father Timmy O'Dowd (Frank McHugh), a curate at nearby St. Francis.

O'Malley temporarily saves the parish from imminent collapse when he sells a song he wrote, "Swinging On A Star," and has Max the music publisher (William Frawley) place the payment in the collection box after a Fitzgibbon sermon pleading with the congregation to be generous in their weekly donation. Just when things begin to brighten, a fire destroys St. Dominic's, forcing Fitzgibbon and O'Malley to begin from scratch. Again, Father Chuck comes to the rescue. He sends the boys' choir on a concert tour starring his old girlfriend from East St. Louis, soprano

Jennie Tuffle now Genevieve Linden (Rise Stevens), a star of the Metropolitan Opera. The income from their successful effort goes to the rebuilding of the church.

As the movie reaches its conclusion, parishioners gather to listen to Father Fitzgibbon's farewell tribute to Father O'Malley in the basement of the burned-out church. During the old priest's talk, the boy's choir begins to sing "Too-Ra-Loo-Ra-Loo-Ral," as his mother, brought over from Ireland by Father O'Malley, proceeds to the altar, and embraces her emotionally overcome son. In the midst of this tearful scene, O'Malley quietly departs through the winter snow–though a year later, he would bring his charm and organizing talents back to the screen to save another parish in McCarey's *The Bell's of St. Mary's.*

There is no doubt that *Going My Way* is frequently hokey, sentimental, and contrived, and it leaves many interesting questions unanswered. For instance, what are East Saint Louis natives O'Malley and O'Dowd, his successor as curate at St. Dominic's, doing in the priest-filled archdiocese of New York? Surely, local fix-it talents could have been assigned to St. Dominic's. And how in the world did old Mrs. Fitzgibbon sail from Ireland to New York through an ocean infested with German submarines? Neither ships nor planes transported ordinary civilians across the Atlantic during World War II.

Despite its excessive sentimentalism and logical flaws, *Going My Way* suited the entertainment and emotional needs of a nation that had recently emerged from a massive economic depression to confront the anxieties, pains, and casualties of war in Europe and Asia. The acting was supberb; the script was clever, often humorous; and the lyrics and music by Burke and Van Heusen pleasant, if not sensational. The dean of popular singers, Crosby, the country's number one movie box-office draw, and the leading opera soprano, Stevens, sang both the secular and religious songs with skill and sensitivity.

Going My Way emphasized the positives of American Catholicism and the lives of its priests, while avoiding the negatives. I recall that one of my professors at St. Ambrose College, Father Edward Catich, complained that McCarey's film did not show the routine drudgery of clerical life: the demoralizing impact of listening to repetitious sins in hot summer and drafty winter confessionals, visiting sick beds, dispensing last rites, burying the dead, attending countless meetings of parish organizations, counseling troubled souls and partners in unhappy marriages, in addition to collecting and managing parish funds. And it did not reveal the loneliness of the celibate life and the confrontations with religious doubts—problems that could, and frequently did, lead to alcohol abuse. *Going My Way* also neglected the difficulty of practicing Catholicism influenced by Irish puritanism and authoritarianism. Neither priests nor the laity found it easy to go Father Chuck O'Malley's way.

In *Bare Ruined Choirs*, Gary Wills conceded that in many ways *Going My Way* was true to the 1940s American Catholic way of life, especially in regard to the clergy. But he found that reality largely negative. Father O'Malley represented priests inadequately trained in the seminary. Their intellectual grasp of theology was limited, a matter of a narrow memorized catechism rather than a thoughtful Thomism. Once in the parish, they functioned more as financiers than as spiritual leaders.[3] J.F. Powers's short stories and Edwin O'Connor's novel *The Edge of Sadness* offer fictional portraits that emphasize the worldly and managerial aspects of clerical life, concerns that interfered with

3. Gary Wills, *Bare Ruined Choirs* (New York: Doubleday & Company, 1972), pp. 22–23.

and often eroded its spiritual dimensions. As the narrator of O'Connor's novel realized, "Any priest in a movie is almost by definition a parody." No doubt Fitzgibbon, "the old Galway-born pastor (cranky but lovable with the wisdom that seems to spring from arthritis)" and O'Malley, "the quaint, pipe-smoking sportsman who, but for the unfortunate fact of his ordination, might well have become a fine second baseman," are idealized clerical stereotypes.[4]

Going My Way nonetheless provided considerable authenticity concerning the flavor of pre-Vatican II Irish-American Catholicism and its impact on other segments of the church. This actuality went beyond the priest as administrator. In reality, the urban wing of the American church was Irish in structure and leadership, and pastoral, rather than theological, in focus. An overwhelming majority of the hierarchy as well as priests, nuns, and brothers were Irish, and they represented the best and brightest of their people. Most of them, like Father Chuck, were true to their vocations, had a powerful impact on the social and cultural, as well as the religious, life of the people they served, and enjoyed enormous respect from the laity. O'Malley fit Mary Gordon's description of the priest of her childhood: "erotically charged yet unreachable . . . who could contain in himself the whole world . . . theoretically available to all, and yet available to no one, just as the Church was in theory open to all and in theory welcoming to all. . . ."[5] And St. Dominic's, with its heavy mortgage, was typical of numerous parishes in post-Depression America.

Beyond the entertainment that it provided to audiences, *Going My Way* played a role in changing public attitudes

4. Edwin O'Connor, *The Edge of Sadness* (Boston: Little, Brown and Company, 1961), pp. 105–106. O'Connor does not specifically mention *Going My Way* in this section of the novel, but it is clear that is the movie to which he refers.
5. Mary Gordon, "Getting Here From There: A Writer's Reflection on a Religious Past," in *Spiritual Quests: The Art and Craft of Religious Writing*, ed. William Zinsser (Boston: Houghton Mifflin Company, 1988), pp. 32–33.

toward Catholics and their religion. Anti-Catholicism was at the core of American nativism. From its beginnings, most people in the United States believed that superstitious followers of authoritarian popery could never be loyal citizens. Catholic religious convictions contradicted liberal democratic institutions and values. Their presence was a subversive political and cultural danger as well as religious threat. The priest, by his clerical garb, his use of Latin in the liturgy, his function of confessor in a secret-filled box at the back of the church, and his celibacy symbolized the alien personality of Catholicism. As late as 1928, fears of Roman influence, power, and intrigue resonated in the presidential election. White-robed, face-hidden Ku Klux Klansmen, especially in the South and parts of the Midwest, marched openly through cities and towns and burned crosses on Catholic lawns. Even thoughtful and respectable people feared that the election of Al Smith would be the equivalent of placing Pope Pius XI in the White House.

Catholics reacted to nativist hostility with a defensiveness that often reached paranoid proportions. Parish and neighborhood enclaves, and Catholic education from the elementary through the university levels as well as other health and social institutions, reinforced a separate Catholic subculture. Although zealous in their love for America, and grateful for the benefits it bestowed, many Catholics found it impossible to believe that they would ever be part of their country's mainstream. Unfortunately, too many of them did not want to be.

In the 1930s, the position and status of American Catholics experienced positive shifts. With other Americans they shared the economic and psychological trauma of the depression—but with so many in stable occupations that persisted through hard times (railroad workers, civil servants, policemen and firemen, teachers, and nurses), the Irish probably endured the Depression better than many other groups. Catholics, usually led by Irish political machines, along with Jewish- and African-Americans and southerners, were an important segment of the coalition that elected Franklin D. Roosevelt president in 1932. He rewarded them with a fair share of political appointments, including a place on the Supreme Court. Irish Catholic congressmen and senators were prominent spokespersons and champions of FDR's domestic and foreign policies. During World War II, Catholics enhanced their patriotic prestige by enthusiastically enlisting in various branches of the armed forces—a phenomenon also chronicled in such films as the 1944 *The Fighting Sullivans.*

Despite the improved status of Catholic Americans, their religion was still suspect, and they continued to feel uncomfortable and insecure. Movies did much to lessen the religious dimension of American nativism. For many non-Catholic Americans, *Going My Way* and its stars, Crosby and Fitzgerald, and other movies featuring such famous Hollywood personalities as O'Brien and Tracy playing Irish-American priests provided a new perspective on Catholicism.[6] Those who were convinced that it was an alien, subversive force and its clergy missionaries of ignorance and superstition saw on the screen a contradiction of their opinions. Moviegoers seldom witnessed the devotional side of Catholicism. Instead, Irish-American movie priests were manly, common-sense social

6. In 1944 another important film about a priest appeared on American screens. In *Keys of the Kingdom*, Gregory Peck played Father Francis Chisholm, a Scottish missionary in China. It was Peck's second movie and made him a cinema favorite. In addition to Pat O'Brien as Father Francis Duffy, the real chaplain of the *Fighting 69th* New York Irish regiment, Preston Foster played the real life navy chaplain, Father Ignatius Donnelly in *Guadalcanal Diary* (1943). For further information on the Irish priest in American movies, see Joseph M. Curran, *Hibernian Green on the Silver Screen: The Irish and American Movies* (Greenwood: Westport, CT, 1989); and Charles R. Morris, *American Catholic: The Saints and Sinners Who Built America's Most Powerful Church* (Random House: New York, 1997), pp. 196–217.

workers guiding their flocks, young and old, in righteous ways, saving bodies as well as souls, emphasizing American cultural values as well as Catholic morality. In war movies, the heroic chaplains were usually Irish-American priests, further asserting the patriotism of their people.

If movies featuring Irish-American priests influenced people of other faiths to feel more comfortable with the Catholic presence, the popularity of these films, particularly *Going My Way* and *The Bells of St. Mary's,* also lifted Catholic egos. It encouraged a belief that they actually might soon be first-class citizens in the country they loved. Growing self-confidence energized religious commitments. Following World War II, large numbers of Catholic men and women decided to become priests, nuns, and brothers; many were ex-soldiers, sailors, and marines. There can be little doubt that *Going My Way,* with its exaltation of the religious life and the priest as hero, contributed to the era's massive increase in religious vocations. For a long time, seminary recreation rooms throughout the country showed it to candidates for Holy Orders, and I personally know of at least one Jesuit college president who entertained at student-faculty convocations with his rendition of "Swinging on a Star."

Some contemporary observers of Catholicism have decided that *Going My Way* has lost relevance. In a recent *Commonweal* article, Dennis O'Brien argues that McCarey's film preaches delayed gratification and working for happiness in a future life rather than present existence —values that conflict with today's focus on instant gratification, particularly in the youth culture.[7] In making his point, O'Brien contrasts *Going My Way*'s Tin Pan Alley music and lyrics with those that rock musicians play and sing. The title song, "Going My Way," as well as

7. Dennis O'Brien "Going which way? Catholicism and pop culture," *Commonweal,* (special section), 22 September 1995, pp. 10–13.

"The Day After Forever" and "Swinging on a Star," not to mention the religious hymns in the movie, all deliver a moral message. They urge self-sacrifice and moral discipline, especially in matters of sex. And they promise that self-control and decency will eventually result in a spiritual contentment that is far more important than material success. O'Brien maintains that present-day young people have little confidence in the future; they are quite cynical about the violent, materialistic, constantly transforming world around them. They soothe their insecurities by living for the moment, and enjoying the thrill and pleasures of sex and drugs. Rock music both expresses and symbolizes the mood and values of our time; O'Brien suggests that the rock song best typifying the generational shift between *Going My Way* and our time is Fleetwood Mac's "Go Your Own Way."

O'Brien holds that the meaningful content of many rock lyrics is miniscule, but believes that the sound rather than the words express the disillusionment, frustrations, and nihilism of the times. Yet, though it is not the music he prefers, he finds a dimension of mystery in rock that potentially contains more spirituality than the messages on morality and cultural uplift found in *Going My Way*. When contrasted with today's complexities, confusion, and doubts, Father Chuck O'Malley's religious way seems too simple and his version of the priesthood too remote—and too sexually neuter—from the realities of life's lonely and difficult journey. O'Brien sees more than sex and drugs in heavy-metal music, and advises Christians to try to understand the appeal of rock and to expand the spiritual possibilities that it contains.

O'Brien's observations concerning the contemporary relevance of *Going My Way* and its hero, Father Chuck

O'Malley, may well be true. Maybe it is a film of the past out of tune with the present; but maybe not. Among older viewers, McCarey's effort still stirs emotions and memories for those who feel nostalgia for a church they grew up in and to their eyes and ears no longer exists, apparently destroyed by a post-Vatican II liturgical disaster. They agree with Mary Gordon, who in commenting on present-day Catholic services, quotes Gertrude Stein's description of Oakland, California: "There is no there there."[8]

Present-day students have erased my earlier doubts concerning *Going My Way's* relevance. During the showings in Loyola University of Chicago's film theater there were hushed and respectful silences. When I turned on the lights I saw tears in the eyes of a few of the young women. All members of the class told me how much they enjoyed the story, the acting, the voice of Bing Crosby, and the songs that he sang. Is it only for entertainment reasons that they preferred it to the other films on the class menu? Or did it stimulate a curiosity and fascination, if not envy, about a time when Catholicism, despite its guilt-ridden anxieties, seemed to guarantee ethical certitudes; when the church's liturgy and sacraments offered emotional and psychological securities; when the Mass and popular devotions provided history and mystery to mundane lives; and when the images of nuns and priests were much more positive than today? *Going My Way* is a limited, sometimes exaggerated document that provides insight into a stage on the way to Irish America's success and respectability. It was a time of extreme limitations, but its religious dimension provided shelter, security, and spiritual solace to people who still were not sure of their position on the American social landscape.

---

8. Gordon, p. 52.

Broadenings

Thomas B. O'Grady

ᕫ

The Ó Bruadair Inheritance:
Some Left a Name Behind Them

"Up Tipp!" my great-aunt Nellie would shout, even late in her life when I first visited her in Clara, County Offaly, and her memory-filled mind had begun to drift. Official records at the Custom House in Dublin say that she was born in Portumna, in the eastern part of County Galway, but one of her favorite stories was of the time her father took her to a hurling match and became so excited that he threw—or as she put it, "pegged"—his hat into the air. Her father was a Tipperary man for sure, and her brother—my father's father—claimed as his birthplace the crossroads village of Toomevara, not far the heart of the heart of that hurling-mad county. Eventually, the family settled in Clara, where my great-grandfather, a harness-maker by trade, found steady work at the Goodbody factory; my paternal grandfather and grandmother both emigrated from Clara to New York City. My father, who was born in Manhattan, in turn emigrated north of the border to Prince Edward Island more than a half-century ago. I was born and grew up on the Island but have settled, apparently permanently, in Massachusetts; four of my six siblings, too, have dispersed as if at the four winds' will. God only knows where our children, and our children's children, will end up as this familial diaspora continues.

In *Ulysses,* James Joyce constructs an elaborate conceit comparing the Irish experience and that of the Lost Tribes of Israel, and at times I have found that analogy disquietingly apt for my own family's nomadic movement over several generations. In fact, struck by a story my father told me about the central role the family phonograph played in his immigrant Irish home on Manhattan's east side, I composed my own conceit about how recordings by the Sligo fiddler Michael Coleman or the Irish tenor John McCormack might represent the Ark of the Covenant for a newly displaced people:

> Though common as a steamer trunk upended deep
> in steerage, taking space, that Edison Victrola
> seemed a cubit-measured casket for plates
> of black shellac encased in upright
> shelves below the crank-wound works.
> Tempered tablets etched in finespun
> whorls like fingerprinted code, those
> waxen disks composed a tabernacled
> covenant for homesick exiles
> fixed in heartsore hope before
> the upraised lid.[1]

I like to think that, in many respects, that poem fits the description Seamus Heaney has applied to "Digging," the famous opening poem of his first volume, *Death of a Naturalist*: "a big coarse-grained navvy of a poem."[2] I did indeed build this poem, titled "East Side Story," to carry a lot of weight—the combined weight of personal, familial and tribal history. But I hope that, like Heaney's in its far

---

1. Unless otherwise indicated, all quotations from my poems refer to the versions published in *What Really Matters* (McGill-Queen's University Press, 2000).
2. Seamus Heaney, "Feeling Into Words," in *Preoccupations: Selected Prose 1968-1978* (New York: Farrar Straus Giroux, 1980), p. 43.

more subtle way, my poem–concluding wistfully with "Holding at forearm's length an old recording / I can almost feel my father's father / link his arm with mine"– also works a variation on the theme (really, more apologia than apology) that W. B. Yeats addresses in the prefatory poem to his volume *Responsibilities* (1914): "I have nothing but a book, / Nothing but that to prove your blood and mine."[3]

So doing, "East Side Story" not only expressed my desire but, in its own way, fulfilled that desire to link myself both to my father's boyhood world of New York City in the 1930s and to a larger sense of my Irish and Irish-American heritage on the paternal side of my family. Perhaps an overly ambitious lyric, it was–I now suppose– my own attempt at "going down and down / For the good turf," as Heaney puts it.[4] Describing my father's telling of the story of how his father's fellow Irish immigrants, some of them friends and relatives from Clara, would visit on Sunday afternoons and end up linking arms and swaying as they gave themselves up to the "familiar / tunes and tones" played on the Victrola, I attempted in composing that poem to be both epic and nostalgic: I attempted both to recuperate "the spirit of longlost / place and time" and to locate myself in close proximity to it, in part by discovering or uncovering the similarities between and among my father's experience of exile from New York City, his father's experience of exile from Ireland, and my own experience of exile from Prince Edward Island.

Well . . . as the old World War I marching song has it, "It's a long way to Tipperary." A member of the King's Liverpool regiment during the Great War, my father's

3. W. B. Yeats, "Introductory Rhymes," in *The Collected Poems of W. B. Yeats,* ed. Richard J. Finneran (New York: Collier Books, 1989), p. 101.
4. Seamus Heaney, "Digging," in *Death of a Naturalist* (New York: Oxford University Press, 1966), p. 14.

father no doubt sang that song with heartfelt gusto; and although the impulse behind "East Side Story" rings no less true to me now than when I was writing the poem, what I ultimately discovered was that the details of my father's experience of exile were not mine, just as the details of his father's experience were not his. This was a poignant enough revelation in itself, as it heightened my sensitivity to how my three daughters—even though they get to spend meaningful time on PEI each year—will have an experience of growing up and moving on utterly unlike mine. More important, it directly challenged an assumption I had internalized: that my primary identity was connected directly to my Irish heritage—through my father and his parents. What was I, and who was I, if not "Irish"?

Well . . . as Oscar Wilde's Algernon Moncrieff observes, "The truth is rarely pure and never simple,"[5] and perhaps even more important again, "East Side Story" held at least part of the answer to the very question—the very disconcerting question—that it raised. For in describing that moment when "my father, from the doorway, watched / in wonder as his father touched the stylus / to a well-worn groove," and, more to the point, in recognizing that at that moment my grandfather and my father were as literally as possible living "between two worlds," I had actually inscribed the truth, neither pure nor simple, of my own predicament: I too was living, as that old harness-maker, my great-grandfather, might have put it, idir dhá shaolta. I too was living, as that Irish root saol allows, not just between two worlds in all of their spatial, temporal, material, and experiential density, but really between two complex states of being: one decidedly grounded in Ireland by way of Irish America, the other just as decidedly grounded in my birthplace and my land of youth, Prince Edward Island.

5. Oscar Wilde, *The Importance of Being Earnest* (London: Dawsons of Pall Mall, 1969), p. 18.

The immediate result of this revelation was that I began to resist my impulse toward writing "Irish" poems. My first two published poems, both on Irish subjects, had appeared in *Poetry Ireland Review and Studies: An Irish Quarterly Review*, and I actually worried that I might be mistaken by some readers as a bona fide "Irish poet"–or, even worse, as a pretender to such a designation. Liberated into an ignorance akin to that which John Montague attributes to the influence that Patrick Kavanagh had on later Irish poets[6]–that is, released from a potentially crippling self-consciousness about the "Irishness" of my poems–I suddenly felt fully licensed to turn toward a dimension of my life that I had taken totally for granted in every respect: in every respect, that is, except as providing the raw material for poems. In short, I discovered my identity as one of the rarest of all birds, a Prince Edward Island poet.

In the process of writing poems, I also discovered just how deeply embedded my Island roots are, how deeply connected I am not only to the people there–family, friends, and community–and not only to the distinctive cultural fabric knit from the shared history of the dominant Scots, French, and Irish immigrant groups, but also to the very landscape, the seascape too, of the place. As Prince Edward Island-born poet Milton Acorn has mused, "To be born on an island's to be sure / You are native with a habitat."[7] A few years ago, peeling PEI potatoes in my south-of-Boston home for that most American of holiday celebrations, Thanksgiving, I remembered how, in the days before mechanized potato digging and consolidated schooling (days that lasted at least into the 1960s), rural schoolchildren would be released from their classrooms in the autumn to help harvest the Island's famous cash crop;

6. John Montague, "Living Under Ben Bulben," *The Kilkenny Magazine* 14 (1966), 46.
7. Milton Acorn, "I, Milton Acorn," in *The Edge of Home: Milton Acorn from the Island*, sel. Anne Compton (Charlottetown: Island Studies Press, 2002), p. 92.

standing over the sink, inhaling the unmistakable fragrance of rich Island loam on the unwashed potatoes, feeling that familiar soil literally under my fingernails, I experienced a powerful revelation of how truly ingrained in my bones the Island was:

> Summers we'd give thanks to be city born
> and bred when, come mid-August, our country
> cousins trudged two weeks ahead to the stern
> task of learning, the clean-cut drudgery
> of school. Of course, in October we'd curse
> the luck that gave them a fortnight repeal
> of break-knuckle rules—though what could be worse
> than digging potatoes in muck-caked fields?
> Who, in their right minds, would envy that chore,
> and pray—in late November, a thousand
> miles and many years away—to restore
> themselves by the grace of clay-coated hands?
> Elbow-deep in a sack of unscrubbed spuds,
> we swear never to wash off that red mud.

———————

"Thanksgiving" continues to be a transporting poem for me. In confronting my own exile directly—that is, without the emotional filter provided by my father's or his father's experiences—the poem also seems, in hindsight, emblematic of a crucial link that ultimately allowed me to reconcile my Irish and Island identities. For in expressing my relationship with the Island through a memory involving my "country cousins," the poem implicitly invokes first my maternal grandfather, Harold Brothers—the immediate lineal common denominator between me and those cousins—

and secondly, through him, an Irish "ancestor" from whom I have received at least part of my poetic license.

The Irish ancestry of Harold Brothers himself is literally etched in stone, on an impressive Celtic cross, the gravestone of his grandfather in the cemetery of St. Joachim's Roman Catholic Church in Vernon River, PEI:

> In Memory of Thomas Brothers
> died Feb. 18, 1878, AE 82
> A native of Co. Wexford
> Ireland emigrated to this country in 1842
> Requiescat in pace
> Be thou faithful until death
> And I will give thee a crown of life

Like the great majority of Irish immigrants to PEI, Thomas Brothers and his wife Elizabeth O'Dunne (or Dunn) left Ireland before the devastating Famine of the late 1840s. No doubt they experienced the typical hardships of nineteenth-century settlers in the thinly populated, densely wooded British colony. But they seem also to have attained a measure of stability if not prosperity as, according to the 1861 census, they were solidly established in Kings County on leased land in Lot 66 and also held 15 acres of land in neighboring Lot 51. In 1880, Meacham's Atlas shows that the farm of 248 acres in Lot 66 had been transferred to Thomas Brothers's son Patrick, my maternal great-grandfather.[8] Eventually the farm would be handed down to my grandfather's brother, Charles Joseph Parnell Brothers. Known as "Pearl"–born in 1886, he was obviously named for Charles Stewart Parnell–he took more to playing the fiddle than to plowing

---

8. "Meacham's Atlas" is the popular name on PEI for the *Illustrated Historical Atlas of the Province of Prince Edward Island* published in Philadelphia in 1880 by J. H. Meacham & Co.

the land, and was the last of the name to reside on the original Brothers family property.[9]

Pearl Brothers figures, a bit romantically, in a couple of my poems. He appears, for instance, in "A Fiddler's Share," where I see my writing of poems as "a corkscrew twist / of my mother's uncle's vice" of sawing on the fiddle, and also in the third section of a five-part poem titled "Local Matters":

> Ever hear tell of a man who bet
> the farm (& lost) that he'd make
> the harvest moon itself mark time?
>
> "To the devil his due." "He'll face
> the music yet." "Bowing & scraping
> as if to save his damn fool soul."
>
> Or ours. With any luck he'll leave
> us in his debt tonight. Footloose
> & footsore before we're quits.
>
> Pay the fiddler & call the tune!
> *Lord McDonald's. Fill Up the Bowl.*
> Local talent. Step to it, lads!

But his brother Harold—my mother's father—figures even more resonantly in my poetic imagination. Harold, too, played the fiddle, but he left the farm of his own volition and enjoyed a long career as a station agent for Canadian National Railways. When I began to write poems about exile, I recognized right away how his profession might afford a symbol adequate to my predicament: he had no need to wander the world, for in a quite literal

---

9. Much of the information relating to the Brothers family on Prince Edward Island comes from an unpublished typescript written in 1983 by Leah Patricia (Brothers) O'Grady.

sense the world came to him on those "singing rows of cast steel"—a punning phrase I borrowed from James Joyce—extending, seemingly infinitely, in both directions past his comfortably familiar platform. After brief postings in Elmira and in Bear River, he spent the balance of his life in Cardigan, where my mother was born and grew up; that is where I picture him at the end of "Bloodlines," the double sonnet at the start of my collection *What Really Matters.* Having as a child gazed down railroad tracks toward their inevitable vanishing point, and having as an adult gone blindly beyond that point, to that chancy spot "around the bend" where "destiny could lie," I had to concede: "Our grandfather wisely mastered the urge / to wander where parallel lines converge."

Ironically, then, it is through that man, fixed contentedly in place in a small village on Prince Edward Island, that I have found a poetic means to reconcile my seemingly competing, between-two-worlds states of being. Or perhaps not ironically, for various kinds of evidence indicate that Harold Brothers grew up on PEI aware of and comfortable with his own Irishness. Certainly the Celtic cross on his grandfather's grave testifies to a familial pride of origin, and the fact that his younger brother Pearl was named after Parnell reveals that the family kept up on Irish politics in the late nineteenth century. Indeed, Irish heritage may even have been a badge of honor: a family anecdote recounts how as children my grandfather and his siblings were taunted as "Irishers" by Scots-Protestant neighbors around Vernon River. Tellingly, my mother mentioned to me many years ago that the next generation of Brothers children—she and her siblings—were brought up in the twentieth century thinking of themselves as "Irish-Canadian."

Several pieces of material evidence also suggest an Irish texture to my grandfather's life. One item is his personal copy, still held by my mother, of William Carleton's classic 1855 romance *Willie Reilly and his Dear Coleen Bawn.* Dog-eared and coming apart at the bindings, it was obviously a favorite book in the Brothers household. Another, more intriguing item supports the reports of how my grandfather used to tease his children by asking, "Did I ever tell you about how it was when I was a little girl?" He would then produce a remarkable duotone photographic portrait of himself and his brother Pearl, both of them with shoulder-length hair in ringlets and all dolled up in frilly little dresses. Family lore offers several explanations for such getup. One story has it that the Irish-born patriarch, Thomas Brothers, was an infant survivor of the Wexford Rebellion of 1798 and that he brought with him from the old country the practice of dressing up little boys as girls until they were old enough to run from the British authorities who might arrest them as budding rebels and transport them to the Barbados. Another story relates to the Irish folk belief in changelings: boys were the preferred target of the fairies and were thus dressed as girls so that they would not be spirited away and replaced by sickly children.

But the most striking evidence of my grandfather's awareness of his Irishness may be both less tangible and less traceable to a specific moment of recognition on either his part or mine. All I know is that somewhere along the way, long before I had developed a distinct interest in either matters Irish or matters poetic, I understood that my grandfather's uncommon surname—my mother's maiden name, Brothers—derives from a just-as-uncommon Irish surname, Ó Bruadair, and that the best-known bearer of that name was a seventeenth-century Irish poet, Dáibhí Ó Bruadair.

The first poem of Dáibhí Ó Bruadair's that I ever read was "A Glass of Beer," James Stephens's frequently reprinted version of "*Seirbhíseach seirgthe*," which I happened upon under its original title, "Righteous Anger," in Frank O'Connor's *A Book of Ireland*, a little anthology I read during my undergraduate days at the University of Prince Edward Island in the mid-1970s. Mentioning that Stephens "ascribe[s] the original poem to David O'Bruadair,"[10] O'Connor planted the seed in my mind for an essay I would write more than two decades later, a detailed exegesis of the poem's provenance that explained Stephens's inadvertent bowdlerizing of the bawdy original.[11] But that undertaking itself coincided exactly with my own first attempt at producing an English-language "version," not quite a translation, of Ó Bruadair's verses. I freely admit that my Irish is virtually all dictionary-based and that whatever "fluency" I achieve comes after I have grappled with mere vocabulary. But I keep good company in admitting this: many years after he published his "translations" of Ó Bruadair and other Irish-language poets in *Reincarnations* (1918), James Stephens confessed in a letter to James Joyce: "I know English and no more. I tried to break into Irish and French, but got not much further than the front-door-mat in either."[12] Drawn to the Gaelic poet by the putative family tie, I had become fascinated with his vision by way of Michael Hartnett's *Ó Bruadair*, an engaging translation of a small selection of Ó Bruadair's lyrics published by Gallery Books in 1985. I subsequently purchased from Greene's Bookshop in

10. Frank O'Connor, *A Book of Ireland* (Glasgow: Fontana/Collins, 1974), p. 222.
11. Thomas B. O'Grady, "Bowdlerizing the Bawdy: Translations of Dáibhí Ó Bruadair's 'Seirbhíseach seirgthe'," *New Hibernia Review* 1, 3 (Autumn, 1997), 62-72.
12. *Letters of James Stephens*, ed. Richard J. Finneran (London: The Macmillan Press Ltd., 1974), p. 371.

Dublin a used copy of the three-volume dual-language edition of Ó Bruadair's work edited and translated by John C.
MacErlean, S.J., published between 1910 and 1917 by the
Irish Texts Society. Mainly as an exercise—a sort of priming
of my own poetic pump during a dry spell—I started to
page through the MacErlean volumes, keeping an eye out
for interesting or curious or singular words, ideas, phrases,
or stances that might invite me to try my hand at rework-
ing them. What I did with what I found continues to
please me:

PREROGATIVE
   after Ó Bruadair

Duty demands it, so just
for the record, I'll venture
this gambit, have a word
with the bride. Like mother,
like daughter, sweet blooms
on soft branches, fair's fair
for the poet where customs abide.

Even flim-flamming shysters
she greets with forbearance;
to thimblerig chancers she grants
tribute too. Furtive glances
disclose here's my turn
to be forward: verses tickling
her fancy, I'll ask for what's due![13]

In this case, what I found, in a brief section of a lengthy
epithalamion—"*Iomdha scéimh ar chur na cluana*"—was

13. "Prerogative" was first published in *The Fiddlehead*, No. 186 (Winter 1995), p. 29.
It was reprinted in *Anthology of Magazine Verse & Yearbook of American Poetry*
(1997 edition).

the intriguing notion of the professional poet's obvious expectation of a "tribute payment" for his contribution to the festive occasion of a marriage.[14] I was especially taken with Ó Bruadair's rhetorical strategy of invoking the bride's mother as a paragon of hospitality and generosity that the bride herself might emulate. Despite collapsing the original four *ranns*–quatrains, in this instance composed in the traditional Irish meter known as *snéadh-bhairdne*–into two seven-line free verse strophes, my version remains more or less faithful to the basic rhetorical structure of the original. While more colloquial than formal, the common expressions that I use–"Duty demands it," "just for the record," "Like mother, like daughter," "fair's fair"–seem to me a reasonable-enough facsimile of the highly conventional diction that defines much poetry in Irish. Ultimately, though, I was intrigued by Ó Bruadair's phrase "*cairt chluana*" and all that it connotes–or actually denotes: every shade of "beguilement" from simple flattery to unscrupulous seduction. By coincidence, only a week or so after I had completed "Prerogative" in the Spring of 1994, I met the author of a Harvard dissertation on Ó Bruadair's two extant epithalamia, and she sent me an article[15] she had written on the root of *chluana*–the word *cluain*–which utterly affirmed my retooling of MacErlean's rather innocent translation of cairt chluana as "a scroll beguiling" (*DDUB* I: 99): attuned to the "verbal philandering and showing-off" that Seamus Heaney associates with poetry written in Irish,[16] an alert reader might well hear in that phrase about "verses tickling / her fancy" the intended reverberation of verses "tickling her fanny"!

14. *Duanaire Dháibhidh Uí Bhruadair/The Poems of David Ó Bruadair*, ed. and trans. John C. MacErlean, S.J., 3 Vols. (London: Published for the Irish Texts Society, 1910, 1913, 1917),Vol. I, pp. 88-117; hereafter cited parenthetically, thus: (DDUB, I: 88-117).
15. Margo Griffin-Wilson, "Cluain agus Cluanaire," Proceedings of the Harvard Celtic Colloquium 9 (1989), pp. 11-30.
16. Seamus Heaney "The Poems of the Dispossessed Repossessed," in *The Government of the Tongue: Selected Prose, 1978-1987* (New York: The Noonday Press, 1990), p. 34.

Thus began my up-close-and-personal poetic engagement with Dáibhí Ó Bruadair, an engagement that has informed my subsequent writing of poems in various crucial respects. Not the least of these involves the utter confidence—nay, arrogance—that Ó Bruadair evinces with regard to his stature as a professional poet. Born in Munster around 1625—both the place and the year of his birth are disputed—he was evidently trained in the tradition of the bardic schools that flourished in Ireland from before the coming of Christianity until the completion of the Tudor conquest in the seventeenth century. A master of the elaborate meters and the highly stylized rhetorical constructions of Irish-language poetry (he seems to have been solidly grounded in Latin and English as well) and a brimming font of arcane historical, literary, and genealogical knowledge, Ó Bruadair apparently enjoyed the patronage of many propertied Gaelic Catholic families in the border area of Counties Cork and Limerick. Composing not only epithalamia but dozens of panegyrics and encomia as well as religious verses, witty satires, and political commentaries, he clearly earned his keep. He also rightfully earned James Stephens's evaluation of him as "one of the most interesting, tormented, angry and eloquent bards I have met with,"[17] and the next piece of Ó Bruadair's verse that I was compelled to rework into English, a year or so after writing "Prerogative," registered all of those qualities. Reconstructed as two slight quatrains, this single *rann* extracted from a much longer poem (*DDUB* I: 29) records the humiliation and the dejection of the entitled poet who has fallen from a position of privilege to mere laborer's status with the collapse of the Gaelic political and social order in the late seventeenth century:

17. Letters of James Stephens, p. 231.

Thirst troubles my task,
    this plowing alone—
in time of abundance
    that tool lay unknown.

Now bruised to the bone
    by a clay-laden blade,
my fingers grow numb
    on the haft of a spade.

Regularly afflicted by poetic self-doubt—constantly aware of "what little I have wrought"—I have to confess that at times I find in the haughty self-assured character of Ó Bruadair a heartening version of the Yeatsian anti-self. More generally, however, I am simply impressed by his capacity to express profound passion, including truly righteous anger, without compromising in the least the integrity of his art.

In fact, it was a combination of that righteous anger—that Swiftian *saeva indignatio*—and a footnote in MacErlean's Irish Texts Society edition that attracted me to forge into English yet another piece of Ó Bruadair's writing. First, I was impressed by the poet's ahead-of-his-time sensitivity regarding domestic abuse in these digressive verses within an elaborate epithalamium. I was also intrigued by his use of the Latin-looking word *pronócum*, footnoted by MacErlean as "an Irish slang word signifying primness, prudery, or affectation": explaining that it is "still a living word in some parts of Ireland," (*DDUB* II:67), MacErlean left it untranslated; I settled on "fawning." But as a Prince Edward Islander with a deeply-rooted appreciation for potatoes, I was most struck by MacErlean's note asserting that Ó Bruadair's use in this poem of the word *potáta* may be "one of the earliest, if not the very earliest, occurrences of the word in Irish" (*DDUB* II: 67):

Only a bully

> rules by the rod
> raising welts
> on his helpmate
> below her brow;
> how kissing
> & fawning
> & new potatoes
> greeted her daily
> before their vows.

Eventually these lines appeared in print along with "Thirst troubles my task" and two other short pieces "*from the Irish of Dáibhí Ó Bruadair,*" under the unifying title "Lines of Descent."[18]

Lines of descent, indeed. Writing in 1975, Michael Hartnett expressed in his powerful poem "A Farewell to English" a personal commitment to writing exclusively in Irish to preserve the almost-lost legacy of the so-called "dispossessed" poets of the seventeenth and eighteenth centuries[19]:

---

18. Thomas O'Grady, "Lines of Descent," *Compost,* 7 (Spring 1996), p. 32.
19. Hartnett eventually revised this commitment, converting it into the project of translating the work not only of Ó Bruadair but also of seventeenth-century poet Pádraigín Haicéad and of early eighteenth-century poet Aodhagán Ó Rathaille. For some thoughts on the implications of Hartnett's undertaking, see my appreciation, "(Re)visiting Michael Hartnett, 1941-1999," *The Irish Literary Supplement,* 19, 1 (Spring, 2000), p. 27.

But I will not see
great men go down
who walked in rags
from town to town
finding English a necessary sin
the perfect language to sell pigs in.

I have made my choice
and leave with little weeping:
I have come with meagre voice
to court the language of my people.[20]

As his publication of *Ó Bruadair* a decade later suggests, Hartnett had Dáibhí Ó Bruadair foremost in his mind, for—as with the poet's birth and his early years—little is known for sure about his last years and his final resting place. That in itself speaks companion volumes to the body of verse he left behind that recorded the decline and the fall of Gaelic Ireland. Feeling especially that many prominent Irish families, both English-speaking as well as Gaelic, had betrayed their traditional culture—the culture that sustained him as a professional poet—in not resisting more vigorously the colonizing British juggernaut, in his later verse Ó Bruadair appears more and more as a self-appointed lightning rod of conscience. In quite different ways, the third and the fourth poems that I included in "Lines of Descent" reflect that role of the poet.

The first of these was Ó Bruadair's caustic response, composed in December of 1688, to the Anglophone Irish transferring their loyalty from James II to the upstart William of Orange. Originally a single freestanding rann (*DDUB* III:114), it seemed to need a looser parceling-out of its linguistic density:

20. Michael Hartnett, *A Farewell to English*, ed. Peter Fallon (Dublin: The Gallery Press, 1978), p. 67.

The rabble turned
their backs on
decency defined,

gambling their prince
for the price
of a vagrant-at-arms,

the same—to my mind,
at day's end—
old sour carry-on:

bedlamite riot round
the tower of Babylon.

While I must admit that the exoticness of the Irish spelling of Babylon—*Baibiolóine*—first drew my attention to these verses, I also appreciated how, capturing the confused and confusing political allegiances of the day, this poem locates Ó Bruadair as the stone in the midst of a world literally changing utterly before his eyes, to borrow a metaphor from Yeats. As such, this poem also forecasts the dissolution of the poet's world that the final poem in the sequence, in its rich ambiguity, poignantly records. Believing that Ó Bruadair addressed his sentiments to a real-life Síle Ní Chorbáin, the Irish Texts Society editor MacErlean nonetheless acknowledges the plausibility of the interpretation advanced by Standish Hayes O'Grady that "this pretty piece 'is considered to be allegorical, Celia, wedded, standing for Ireland fallen away from the good old use and wont'" (*DDUB* III:24). I do not attempt to resolve this debate in rendering the opening rann into free-verse couplets:

Sheila, the cool
& slender; dewy-haired;

prudent swan-flank
breasting the waves:

since queenliness
lords itself on you

I'm ruined, not
knowing whom I see.

In either case—literal or allegorical, "Sheila" as female patron or as Ireland feminized—the poet feels betrayed and abandoned. Clearly, he had begun his line of descent into the virtual oblivion of an unheralded death—apparently in 1698, though his last-known poem dates to 1694—and an unmarked place of burial.

It is at that point, just as he appears to slip between the cracks of history, that I begin to sketch my own "line of descent" from Dáibhí Ó Bruadair. I like to believe that even if diluted by centuries and by oceans, by temperament and by language, the literary bloodline—the consanguinity of spirit with Ó Bruadair that I have felt when working, either as poet or as scholar, with his writing—has some authentic substance. Remotely collateral at best, any literal bloodline with the poet that I might want to claim through my mother's side of the family—the Brothers side—is, of course, untraceable. Yet, in responding several years ago to an invitation to submit to *Landmarks: An Anthology of New Atlantic Canadian Poetry of the Land,* I suddenly saw in the bowed but not quite broken figure of the poet Ó Bruadair, his "fingers grow[n] numb

/ on the haft of a spade," the analogous figure of my Wexford-born great-great-grandfather—or vice versa. "Is mairg do chonnaire an chinneamhain d'éirigh dúinn," Ó Bruadair wrote in a poem addressed to the children of Cúchonnacht Ó Dalaigh (*DDUB* III:4), a fellow poet whose fast-fading repute after his death became a cautionary tale for Ó Bruadair himself: "O pity the one who foreknows his own misfortune."

An illiterate Irish immigrant, Thomas Brothers might be remembered only by the original deed to his land in Lot 66, preserved in the Prince Edward Island Provincial Archives, which bears as a signature his mark "X" next to a variant spelling—Broathers—of his surname. Aligning myself romantically with my literary "ancestor," the beleaguered Irish poet whose words have survived—for now, at least—the proverbial test of time, I might thus have felt unapologetically dismissive toward my literal ancestor, that man who performed the brute-like backbreaking labor of taming the land, of transforming forests into fields, of fields into more fields: "I have nothing but a book, / Nothing but that to prove your blood and mine," indeed.

And yet my poetic reckonings have led me to understand something else about that true-born Irishman, my great-great-grandfather—that he has what "Meacham's Atlas" documented in 1880 and what signposts may well announce until the end of time, a name written into the landscape:

SOME LEFT A NAME BEHIND THEM
—Ecclesiasticus 44:8

HISXMARK on a land agent's
ledger, the only sign my grandfather's
grandfather left behind to link

his life's hardbitten lot to another's
deeply furrowed state of mind. Defter
strokes than that the bard Ó Bruadair

drew to stake his wordstrong claim
to a hearthside seat before disorder
in princely courts spelled spiraling

defeat for the poet's trade. Born
to that exalted craft, not made
for lowbrow labor and mincing scorn

in fields gone wretchedly to weed,
he shouldered the polished tools
of tarnished art down twisted lanes

to an unknown grave. No family jewels
descended from that broken line—nor
lasting fame for one who in his time

commanded by mere verse respect
from all who knew the power of rhyme
to make or break the rank of house,

sept, or tribe in history's long parade:
no more to show for upright toil
than a hireling bent upon a spade.

No more, I thought, *than that unlettered
farmer*–my stooped ancestor– . . . until
the day a hardly traveled graveled route

set straight as a master plowman's drill
my straying sense of worth and wealth:
that blind belief in how the ages weigh

and measure lives by momentous deeds
performed as if for permanent display–
heroic feats or acts of epic derring-do,

mountains moved, bridges built or burned,
the world remade by monumental will.
How else might immortality be earned?

"O pity the one who foreknows his own
misfortune. . . ." *Yet that* poem survives,
and now thin-blooded generations on,

abashed at how, for years, on Sunday drives,
I passed by that unposted byway,
ignorant of the man who uprooted rock

and stump from acres of stubborn soil,
I take hopeful heart in taking stock
of what remains in an open book.

In *Meacham's Atlas*–Lot 66–I trace
that which, indelibly etched, endures:
Brothers Road . . . much more name than place.[21]

21. *Landmarks: An Anthology of New Atlantic Canadian Poetry of the Land,* ed. Hugh
MacDonald & Brent MacLaine (Charlottetown, PEI: The Acorn Press, 2001), pp. 119-20.

A century-and-a-quarter after his death, Thomas Brothers still has his Celtic cross standing tall on his grave. And he has far more than that, I realize, reflecting on my own unsure exile's hold on Prince Edward Island—a claim I once described as "a fingerhold (and no more) / on a solid sandstone shore."

AÍFE MURRAY

∾

A YANKEE POET'S IRISH HEADWATERS

On a day alternating sun and spit, I circled a mountain at the far reaches of South Tipperary that rises humpback from the farmscape. The Golden Vale it's called, a swath of fertile country by the River Anner, the lands of Ballypatrick and Sliabh na mBan ("Mountain of the Women"). To the west lies Killusty, a blackened churchyard at a curve in the road, and, on the north face, Killurney farmhouses hug a slope above Kilcash. In September, 2000, I traveled nine thousand miles to glimpse this mountain, a place of "origins" for a well-known American poet. Not her own lineage, exactly, but one she pointed to by a series of oblique gestures—of those who had made possible, in Seamus Heaney's words, "a course for the breakaway of innate capacity."[1]

From the medieval walls behind P. J. Lonergan's pub in Fethard it is possible to take a long view across the Vale to Sliabh na mBan (in a nostalgic ballad, the Valley of Sweet Slievenamon). This is where I found myself contemplating the headwaters of Emily Dickinson's "long summons into the vocation of poetry."[2] South Tipperary

---

1. Seamus Heaney, *The Redress of Poetry* (London and Boston: Faber and Faber, 1995), p. 15. I wish to thank Denise Meagher and the Tipperary Rural and Business Development Institute for making possible a visit to County Tipperary, and to thank my companions on an extraordinary sojourn in the Golden Vale.
2. Kathleen Fraser, *Translating the Unspeakable: Poetry and the Innovative Necessity* (Tuscaloosa and London: The University of Alabama Press, 2000), p. 10.

is a countryside so ample with poets and scholars that some nineteenth-century farmers were known to converse in Latin and Greek, and, by candlelight, to study Irish manuscripts. James Stephens wrote admiringly of the erudite farmers he met while sojourning in this part of nineteenth-century Ireland. At Nine Mile House, the Meagher family held literary evenings in their tavern for three generations. For many hundreds of years the literary sensibility has been honed and made rich as the soil of the Golden Vale itself.[3] Margaret Maher of Killusty and her brother-in-law, Thomas Kelley, from Killurney—two immigrants from the slopes of Sliabh na mBan—made their way in the mid-1850s to Amherst, Massachusetts where they became long-term servants for the family of Emily Dickinson. Each played a significant role in the life of the renowned American poet.

Eleven years after her mistress had been laid in the grave—by six Irish laborers whom Dickinson knew well and requested for pallbearers—maid Margaret Maher was asked if she had anything to do with Dickinson's poems, how and where they were kept. She replied, "She kept them in my trunk. . . .They were done up in small booklets, probably twelve or fourteen tied together with a string."[4] That this poor laboring woman had intimate knowledge of the exact size and nature of the poet's literary enterprise suggests that Maher was an authority on more than the contents of her trunk. Dickinson had not only trusted her maid with the fruits of her labor, but had also asked her to burn the poems when she died. Maher broke the apparent deathbed oath, appealing tearfully to Dickinson family members, and, thus, the manuscripts

3. James Maher, *Slievenamon in History, Folklore, and Song: a Tipperary Anthology* (Tralee: Kerryman, 1954) p. 12; Eoghan Ó Néill to author, undated letter, 1996.
4. Deposition of Margaret Maher, Witness Called by the Plaintiff, Lavinia N. Dickinson v. Mabel Loomis Todd et al., The Commonwealth of Massachusetts, Hampshire County Superior Court, 1897, p. 13.

were saved.[5] Dickinson also honored Tom Kelley by requesting that he be her chief pallbearer. Her life and writings have been studied with precision and yet these signs have escaped notice; in the well-trod Dickinson story, the many permanent and seasonal servants have been overlooked.

Kathleen Fraser asks if there is a genetic propensity for making poetry; are some born into poetic language "as if the mind were waiting like a large empty page to be imprinted with the intaglio markings of the world crowding foreword to make its impress?"[6] The *intaglio markings* of Dickinson's first language came not just at her mother's breast but in the soothing arms of a maid who helped ease life in the early years of family increase. Most of those first family servants, often hired intermittently for specific tasks, were local African Americans and itinerant white workers from Vermont.[7] The young Emily would have spent much of the day with them, playing with dolls underfoot in the kitchen while the maid cooked or crouched in the barn, studying the stableman's fingers and his quiet words to the cow. When the children reached school age, the family got by mostly on their own efforts with the short-term assistance of helpful relatives and hired help. By their socially active teenage years, Emily and her sister, Lavinia, rebelled against the ongoing demands of labor-intensive work necessary to maintain their prominent family. For Emily, too, the press of language was already exerting itself. In the face of their daughters' resistance—and the changing habits at midcentury of middle- and upper-class families—the Dickinsons hired their first permanent maid. Even with the hiring of a permanent maid, Emily and

5. Martha Dickinson Bianchi, *Emily Dickinson Face to Face* (Boston: n.p., 1932), pp. 59–60. See also Aífe Murray, "Miss Margaret's Emily Dickinson," *Signs: Journal of Women and Culture and Society* 24 (3), 1999: 697–732.
6. Fraser, *Translating the Unspeakable*, p. 8.
7. James Avery Smith, in conversation, January 28, 2000.

Lavinia were still expected to contribute at home and did so, side by side, with servants. Emily remained the family bread and dessert composer, author of jams and wine. For someone following a thread of linguistic clues, the daily rhythm of servant talk and work-noise became "indelibly marked" in the poet's memory.[8]

What I discovered by studying Dickinson's periods of literary productivity is that there was a sharp upswing in the poetic production after the family hired its first long-term permanent maid, Irish immigrant Margaret O'Brien. Having a permanent maid opened a window of opportunity for Dickinson that enabled her to identify herself as a poet.[9] Her most prolific writing period is framed by O'Brien's 1856–1865 tenure. When this maid departed for her own kitchen through marriage, the Dickinson household was thrown into domestic upheaval. Dickinson had to assume the cooking of three meals a day and "besides wiping the dishes for Margaret, I wash them now, while she becomes Mrs. Lawler. . . . I winced at her loss because I was in the habit of her, and even a new rolling pin has an embarrassing element, but to all except anguish, the mind soon adjusts."[10] While O'Brien stood at the stove, Dickinson steadily turned out one hundred to three hundred poems a year. In 1865 she crafted two hundred twenty-nine, but with O'Brien's departure by 1866, Dickinson's output dropped to ten poems. And the numbers stayed similarly low for three-and-a-half years of intermittent maids,

8. Walter Benjamin, "Art in the Age of Mechanical Reproduction," quoted in *The Politics and Poetics of Transgression*, ed. Peter Stallybrass, Peter and Allon White (Ithaca: Cornell University Press, 1986), p. 155.
9. Faye Dudden, *Serving Women: Household Service in Nineteenth-Century America* (Middletown, CT: Wesleyan University Press, 1983), pp. 240–41.
10. *The Letters of Emily Dickinson*, ed. Thomas H. Johnson, 3 vols. (Cambridge : Harvard University Press, 1958), letter 311; hereafter cited thus: (*Letters* 311).

until Margaret Maher of Tipperary was wooed to the Dickinson Homestead in 1869.

Maher considered this a temporary post while she waited for word from her brothers, Michael and Thomas, who had already left for the California gold fields. Dickinson's poetic vocation was so strong that she was almost certainly the force behind her father's immediate offer of higher wages as a ploy to retain Maher—against the young woman's own desires and the financial resources of her former employers.[11] A Kelley great-great granddaughter believes her "Aunt Mag" intended to go to California to change her life. She was just turning 28 and had probably labored as a domestic servant since her emigration as a teen. A 1953 article by Jay Leyda reported that after the Maher children emigrated, Margaret returned, "perhaps alone," to accompany their aged parents from Killusty to the new home in America.[12] But Kelley descendants, whom I interviewed in 1994, had never heard of this return voyage. Such a trip seems highly unlikely because of the danger and expense, but the story does reveal the esteem with which Maher was held by both Yankee and Irish Amherst. Dickinson described her maid as "warm and wild and mighty" and "seemed never to tire of defining Maggie's virtues and qualities, for herself as well as for her friends."[13]

When Margaret Maher became a fixture in the brick house on Main Street, Dickinson's literary productivity spiked and remained steady, averaging 75 poems and letters annually (until her final 1884 illness). She recommenced making her handstitched books, the "fascicles" that Maher stored in her trunk. And she did all of this in the companionability of working beside her maid. In fact,

11. Murray, "Miss Margaret's Emily Dickinson," 712–13.
12. Jay Leyda, "Miss Emily's Maggie," in *New World Writing* (New York: New American Library, n.d.), pp. 255–67.
13. *Letters* 907; Leyda, "Miss Emily's Maggie," p. 266.

just months after Maher's arrival, Dickinson must have felt that life at home was now complete for she wrote to Thomas Higginson "I do not cross my Father's ground to any House or town."[14] Not only was she seemingly content not to roam abroad, but there is also evidence that the poet was increasingly drawn to the kitchen, once Maher took up residence. Manuscripts indicate that after 1870 Dickinson was writing more and more on kitchen scraps—bills, the back of recipes, food wrappers—suggesting that her lyrics were originating in domestic climes where Dickinson was often found "baking a loaf cake with Maggie," chatting while they did evening dishes together, or jotting notes for a poem while gazing out the kitchen door at the mid-still of a spring morning.[15] This is how her cousins remember her, cooking brilliant and original dishes and reading her lyrics aloud to them in the confidence of the pantry or from memory in what one cousin referred to as "talking poetry."[16]

In those later years, coinciding with Maher's tenure, the kitchen was not the impediment Dickinson saw it when as a rebellious teenager she was anxious to get out from under many onerous tasks. And her maid became more than someone who invisibly lifted the burden so her mistress could write. I suspect that Maher not only made possible "a course for the breakaway," but was integral to what I call "Dickinson's desire for language."

How did Maher and Kelley, who had such an important effect on Dickinson, get entwined in her story? In the mid-1850s, when life was becoming easier for a certain

14. *Letters* 330.
15. *Letters*, p. 907.
16. Martha Ackmann, "'I'm Glad I Finally Surfaced': A Norcross Descendent Remembers Emily Dickinson," *The Emily Dickinson Journal* 5, 2 (1996), 123.

Amherst poet, but it was deteriorating for the poor of South Tipperary, Thomas Kelley's father Michael Kelly and mother, Margaret (Crowley), were subtenants on the land William O'Donnell leased from the marquess of Ormond.[17] A series of civil laws may have resulted in the family's eviction and hastened Tom Kelley aboard a New York-bound ship in the winter of 1854. He had no idea he would one day figure in the life of one of the world's best-known poets, nor that he would be all but erased from the narrative.

A year after he disembarked in New York harbor, Tom Kelley and Mary Maher were headed by stagecoach through "The Notch" in the Holyoke Range to the nearest Catholic church to be married. They had most likely met at social gatherings in South Tipperary; they may even have been distantly related through the Mahers of Killurney.[18] They settled in an Amherst tenament and Tom, who labored as a hod carrier, might have been hired by Emily's father, Edward, during the extensive 1855 renovations of the Homestead. Edward was the Amherst College treasurer and for many years employed Tom as the school's night watchman. Whatever he did at the Homestead, Tom Kelley was around enough to make an impression on Emily Dickinson. It was on at least one occasion that a distraught poet sought his comfort. When Tom learned that one of Dickinson's dearest friends was mortally stricken, he hastened to her door. "I thought first of you," he said and the poet (as she wrote) "ran to his Blue Jacket and let my Heart break there – that was the warmest place."[19]

Across the Dickinson meadow from the Homestead, nestled between a brow of hill and the train depot, Tom and Mary Kelley leased, and eventually bought, two

17. The spelling of the Kelley family name apparently changed upon immigration.
18. John Quinn and Eoghan Ó Néill in conversation, September 7, 2000, Purcell farm, Ballypatrick, Tipperary, Ireland.
19. *Letters* 752.

houses from Edward Dickinson. In one, the Kelleys raised eight children; in the neighboring one Mary's parents and siblings were housed. With Margaret's financial help, a third house was built at what eventually became known as Kelley Square. This compound, abundant with fruit trees and arbors of roses and grapes, was the center of Kelley family life until the 1940s when, through generational increase and changing times, family members moved to other homes in the region.

Tom and Mary's youngest granddaughter told me that many new immigrants got their foothold in America with her grandfather's help. The newly arrived Irish boarded at the Square where Margaret cooked their meals each afternoon in a break between duties at the Homestead.[20] I spoke to granddaughter Catherine Kelley in July, 1994– her red Ford Fairlane pulled to a curb at midnight on North Prospect Street– and she told me that every Amherst Irish woman in labor was attended by her grandmother. At eighty, Miss Kelley was twice my age, twice as beautiful. She wouldn't agree to see me, though, until she'd made time to have her hair done. Life has a way of working out, she said while insects trilled in wet foliage beyond our open windows. Even the torn edges to my own, she confirmed, would come right.

Three years later, a brisk and brilliant April Sunday, I was back in Massachusetts leading a public walking tour of Amherst. Servants Margaret Maher and Tom Kelley were the focus of a "Dickinson" tour. As nearly two hundred of us stood around Dickinson's grave, we discussed the unexamined fact that she had selected six Irish laborers for her pallbearers. I asked for a show of hands by Tom Kelley's descendants and the arms of more than forty people reached above the crowd.

20. Aífe Murray, "Miss Margaret's Emily Dickinson," 715.

———————

Margaret Maher appears to have been a good match for Dickinson, as much a soulmate as a servant. My guide to South Tipperary, Colonel Eoghan O'Neill, intimated as much when I telephoned him in Wicklow to make arrangements for a visit. He grew up in Lisronagh, the next parish over from the Kellys and Mahers, and we were plotting to visit the Golden Vale in early September, 2000. "I don't consider myself expert in her poetry," he commented in his clipped style, "but she seemed to write a great deal about nature." The Kelleys and Mahers were country people, he reminded me, and would have had an abiding sense of the natural world. Knowing the long literary tradition in South Tipperary, I understood that at some level there was a meeting of minds and sensibilities in the Homestead kitchen.

A bit lost near Killurney, our party—which included Mrs. O'Neill and Niall Dunphy, once a country boy from County Laois—wandered onto the farm of Johnson and Addie Purcell tucked below Slievenamon. They're retired now and have moved into a bungalow, leaving the larger farmhouse for their son's family. As it turned out, Mrs. Purcell and Colonel O'Neill remembered each other from their schooldays. As we sat talking in the parlor we were joined by John Quinn, who recalled Pat Kelly, the last of Tom Kelley's family to be waked in the 1940s out of the family home in Killurney. A while later, Mrs. Purcell invited us to sit for tea at a large square wooden table in the kitchen. I come from a family of excellent bakers, but I don't remember ever having better cakes and breads than on that gusty afternoon in the lee of the Mountain of the Women. Rain tapped the roof and sun burst intermittently through the porch windows as the talk meandered.

It was a day reminiscent of some in my early twenties spent cycling through South Amherst, afternoons when autumn insisted round my collar, when yellow and red leaves pressed in the verge of wet road skirting the Holyoke Range. Later, soaking-in the words and pacing of country people visiting on a changeable Tipperary fall day, my urban self came as close as it possibly can to grasping what it means for lives to be defined by weather. The quickened rhythms of fall, working until one can no longer see, waiting for fields to dry in spring, the havoc of a sudden heat, anxiety of an early frost. "You never lose sight that you're dealing with something on its own terms," concluded a farmer's son.[21] By 1870, in part due to her father's enterprise, Amherst had shifted away from the self-sufficient farming that had formed Dickinson's early life. Because life in the Golden Vale probably resembled the important agrarian rhythms of Dickinson's youth, Maher and Dickinson spoke the same language, one that may have been essential to her art.

It is a soft day, as they say in Ireland, but this time I'm not by green meadows bounding the priest's college in Thurles and marsh-lipped river wending south to Carrick-on-Suir. An early winter is foretold on the horizontal roofs and vertical pavements of San Francisco as I sit indoors listening to the speech of South Tipperary in a dialect that holds still the inflections of the Déise Gaeltacht. It's filling the room from an audio tape sent to me by Michael Coady, grandson of a River Suir boatman. It's his multi-voiced poem "All Souls" spoken by Coady's friends and neighbors. While rain snakes the window pane behind

21. Michael Des Jardines, in conversation, Feburary 4, 2002.

these disembodied voices, I consider their predecessors, one hundred fifty years ago, speaking with Dickinson in her Amherst kitchen. Now, through the distorting mirrors of class and race in America, those men and women who had served and shared the kitchen with Dickinson have become people without substance, looked through rather than at.

Dickinson's poetry brought together the different speech patterns and voices she heard around her. Taking to heart the advice of a housekeeping expert of her day, Lydia Maria Child, the poet gathered up all the fragments so none would be lost–apple peel, paper scraps, and fragments of language.[22] The cooing of an adored childhood maid; the stentorian speech of her lawyering grandfather, father, and brother; exhortations of revivalist preachers; whispers in a darkened bedroom between sisters and cousins; and the flavored talk of admired servants were all "cause for ecstatic response."[23] When Dickinson and her sister divided up the household tasks, she chose baking–a chore that placed her for many hours each day in the creative flux and combustion of her nineteenth-century kitchen. It is not merely that the kitchen was free of the control logic of the Victorian era that worked against the freedom of the imagination–but surely Dickinson's ear metabolized the richness of those who had not "shut their lips on poetry."[24]

Various theories have been proposed as to why Dickinson did not "publish" during her lifetime–although "print"

22. Lydia Maria Child, *The American Frugal Housewife* (Boston: Carter, Hendee and Company, 1832), p. 1. See also Jeanne Holland's excellent article about Dickinson's "domestic technologies" in "Scraps, Stamps, and Cutouts: Emily Dickinson's Domestic Technologies of Publication," in *Cultural Artifacts and the Production of Meaning: The Page, the Image, and the Body,* ed. Margaret Ezell, J. M. O'Keeffe, Catherine O'Brien (Ann Arbor: University of Michigan Press, 1994), pp. 154–55.
23. Fraser, *Translating the Unspeakable*, p. 8.
24. Benedict Kiely, "Dialect and Literature," *The English Language in Ireland,* ed. Diamuid Ó Muirthe (Dublin and Cork: The Mercier Press, 1977), p. 96.

is how she worded it—but preferred sending letters as poems or tucking a few lines beside a cake or bloom for a neighbor. Perhaps she disdained it as the "auction of the mind." It is just as likely, though, that she didn't want to— or couldn't—separate her art from its aura.[25] A work of art has a presence in time and space, and Dickinson seemed reluctant to sever her art from its relations, its embeddedness within a home ritual and tradition. She recognized that the locus of her kitchen, with servants and family, was where "something unhindered, yet directed, [could] sweep ahead into its full potential."[26]

To explain differences between Melville and Dickinson, the New England poet Susan Howe returned to history and geography, saying readers should "trust the place to form the voice." When Howe further commented that "sounds and spirits (ghosts if you like) leave traces in a geography," I wondered if there isn't a more reciprocal interplay of place and voice?[27] That when I first listened to the reversed syntax of Dickinson's poetry my mind was racing "home." When I read her, don't I hear mine call out to me? The Cork of my grandmother, Theresa Lynch Murray; the South Carolinian African-American Vernacular English of childhood friend Martha Miller? Does her language tell me back to myself in what Whitman called America's "voices mysteriously united"?[28] Haven't I found my forebears there—as much as did this Yankee poet from upriver. . . .

As when, a few years back, searching for clues about the Dickinson servants, any scrap of possibility, in Yale

25. Walter Benjamin, "The Work of Art in the Age of Mechanical Reproduction," in *Illuminations: Essays and Reflections* (New York: Schocken Books, 1968), pp. 220–23.
26. Seamus Heaney, *The Redress of Poetry* (London: Faber and Faber, 1995), p. 15.
27. Susan Howe, *The Birth-mark: Unsettling the Wilderness in American Literary History* (Hanover: University Press of New England, 1993) p. 156.
28. Alicia Ostriker, *Stealing the Language: The Emergence of Women's Poetry in America* (Boston: Beacon Press, 1986), p. 8.

library's special collections, I met silence again. In this coastal New England town I knew so well, I wrote of being . . . here in the effluvia that washes down stream, what settles out where it courses to the Sound, kicking stones in that strip of river and shore line by Long Wharf where heat hunkers by cattails and torn up tarmac. Finding them here as anywhere, on the west edge of the town where I grew. Cars whiz past on the highway separating those of us who fish from the awkward rigs turning into Long Wharf. Last place in town one would think to look, be, but this is the map, the artery that empties through Hadley, past Mount Tom, depositing what I sift through. Studying what washes up on this southern Connecticut shore, engines accelerate behind me, two men with cast lines (but I'm sure I would never eat anything out of this water), grey sky hovers the low slung marshy coast. I didn't think I belonged here. But the more I watch the Sound lip higher and over itself, the more I know. . . .

James Liddy

❦

CROESUS AND DOROTHY DAY:
MOON GAFFNEY'S IRISH AMERICA

The passion of Ireland is to talk about people when they are alive; the passion of North America is to discuss people when they are dead, but only on family trees. On the one hand gossip, on the other hand genealogy. In *Moon Gaffney*, one of a number of decisive novels of the late 1940s to mid-1950s, Irish Americans can be seen to do both. The other energy of this group is to carry war against its designated enemies. Because it is New York, the characters are more Irish-American than the Irish Americans themselves so they shoot from the trenches of a militant New World. With their version of the United States as protector, they intend to give no quarter to contemporary opponents. To get at what the novel is trying to do, perhaps I can rephrase my favorite Jacobite Dr. Johnson—patriotism is the last refuge of immigrants and possibly for several generations. The patriotism of this community holds two double swords: one combining church and state; the other, two Atlantic coasts.

I can record two surprising footnotes about Sylvester's *Moon Gaffney* (1947). It was written in Guatemala City. While working on this paper in the University of Wisconsin-Milwaukee's Jeremiah Curtin Hall, I discovered that its author, the Brooklyn writer Harry Sylvester, was the grandson of Jeremiah Curtin (1835–1906)—Lincoln's polyglot consul in Moscow, first scholarly collector of Irish folktales. Surely an irony here: an Irish-American model and mentor and a descendant who uses satirical fiction to dissent from ethnic pieties.

My strategy in identifying the renegade nature of *Moon Gaffney* involves a few heresies of my own, including personal genealogy, that dash of soothsaying proper to a bard and critical commentary. For one of the characters in Harry Sylvester's novel, the most complete villain in fact, is based on a cousin of mine, Eddie Reeves, here called Peter Calahan. There is a lot of nonfiction in the book. Dorothy Day—one of the good people, rather I should say saints, in the plot—appears under her own name. An appearance by Al Smith, recorded as "honest Al," turns into a self-conscious hymn for Irish America. That paean gives a glint of light in the grim portrait of the ruling powers of the city of New York—here termed "The Hall," otherwise Tammany—that political machine that lived, according to Steven Erie, by "the trading of divisible benefits . . . [and] provided loaves and fishes for its followers."[1] Sylvester's method is a glance-by-glance, chat-by-chat, denunciation-by-denunciation, innuendo-by-innuendo demonstration of what it takes to keep and increase power in an atmosphere of plush assimilation rituals and folk snobberies. Yet Sylvester sings, too, of the Emerald re-creation of New York, surely an accomplishment of triumphalism and symbol of the deliverance dreamed of by the Gaelic poets under colonialism.

By moving through several groups of characters at various high social levels, *Moon Gaffney* details this new world of riches. The glittering pageant revealed is a different

---

1. Dennis Clarke, "Organizing in America," *The Irish Literary Supplement* (Spring, 1989), 43.

parade from Mr. Dooley's patch of society. As described by Charles Fanning, Finley Peter Dunne offers "solid and sympathetic characterizations of the common people—the laborers, dray man, and mill workers who make up the working-class immigrant clientele of Mr. Dooley's saloon."[2] Sylvester's fourth novel is set in the 1930s. It gives an unmasked view of the networking, racism, and pious fantasies of a society whose original native conditioning supplied only the start of its power. The rebels are the children of a new upper class who seek and deal with crises of conscience. Beside Moon, the reluctant self-examiner, these avatars for justice include his friends James Kavanagh, the more radical Bart Schneider—whose mother is Irish, hardly good enough—and their girlfriends. Their conflict lies with the umbilical "Hall" and Chancery.

The younger males graduate from Notre Dame or Georgetown, where Calahan makes the decision not to enter the family grocery business. Old and young perform their duties on Sunday—even those inclined to anarchism or communism (the decent guys); the sexes smoke; politicos and their friends eat steak in Italian restaurants; the folks drink as much as my great uncle Paddy Reeves, who said on his death bed, "Thank God, I drank enough alcohol to float the Queen Mary." Paddy had spent most of his life in New York. The good complain about the Pharisees in the Chancery; the majority keep naming "Commies"; the about-to-get-married can be sure of honorable sex shortly.

My mother's paternal uncles and their children lived on or near Central Park. Their social lives were spent in establishments like the Athletic Club. My great uncle James, the wealthy brother of Paddy, also appears in *Moon Gaffney*. Here I will simply align to Sylvester's text part of James's 1935 message to my mother:

2. Charles Fanning, "Finley Peter Dunne and Irish-American Realism," in *Irish-American Fiction*, ed. Daniel J Casey and Robert F. Rhodes (New York: AMS Press, 1979), p. 21.

178

. . . Business conditions here are very bad and not a
bright spot on the horizon. Labor and government
are in firm control and capital is the big bad wolf
whom the place is blamed on for the loss of $50 a
week jobs they had promised themselves.

The next year James apologized for a "small present" of
$100 because Roosevelt was ruining the country. For an
account of the brothers and sisters remaining in Scariff, County
Clare, consult Edna O'Brien's short story "The Savages."

The other elitism at work here is exclusiveness in the
rectory, in the chancery, in the archbishop's house, in all
the environs of St. Patrick's, in the Irish-American clergy
and in the "FBIs," or Foreign-Born-Irish priests. Careers in
the Catholic church and urban politics were the avenues of
upward mobility and assimilation into the American mainstream. These highways were Jansenist highways. A sly
omniscient narrator, Sylvester puts into his characters' dialogue and interior monologues historical explanations such
as the connections of the all-Ireland seminary at Maynooth
with pre-revolutionary France. *Moon Gaffney* is as much a
Catholic novel as it is an Irish-American one, for it is a
tract that displays an obsession with Roman Church
liturgy and routines. As the prologue to Sylvester's John
Fury explains, they brought their priests with them.

The elders of "The Hall" profess themselves worried by
the emergence of "Commie"-type liberalism among young
clerics, especially in the supposedly "red" diocese of Brooklyn, which pays some attention to papal encyclicals on
labor. Sylvester's ambivalent central character, Moon, who
is slowly growing an independence that endangers his position in machine politics, has to visit Hennessy, the court
clerk of Brooklyn, to plead with him to send his daughter

back to her husband, who represents a left-wing labor union. Though Moon is the son of the deputy fire commissioner, who is a friend of Hennessy, he suffers a rant,

> "Our diocesan paper! That ignorant little sheet, run by young twirps of priests. . . . If you read the nonsense in it, the pure, vicious nonsense. Stuff that came to them from some Communist front organization. The same sort of thing that Roosevelt has started to do. Ah, if ever a man betrayed his supporters, betrayed good Irish hearts, he's the one."[3]

The long walk to the Republican suburbs has begun.

The young priest in the Catholic Worker house, incidentally incardinated in the Brooklyn diocese, Fr. Shanahan, exposes his situation:

> "Monsignor Clancy has already requested my removal to another parish. . . . I am, he says, a radical, a Jew-lover, a complete fool . . . he attributes much of my recalcitrance in having been born in this country, to being what he calls an Irish-American. If I were real Irish like him, born in Ireland, I would not have such outlandish ideas." (*MG* 124–25)

The older priests are made of immigrant seminary steel. They dispense no mercy. The Gaffney family pastor Fr. Malone uses the wake of the deputy fire commissioner to press ideology, "My purpose in this brief talk is to let you know that Communism's enemies not only exist but are themselves militant, not only in Europe where the great Mussolini has cast down the gauntlet, but in this very country . . ." (*MG* 202). Fr. Coughlin had many brothers.

---

3. Harry Sylvester, *Moon Gaffney* (1947), 143; hereafter cited parenthetically, thus: (*MG* 143).

The essays in Casey and Rhodes's *Irish-American Fiction* (1979) contain scant reference to Harry Sylvester, though he is included in the long bibliography. William Shannon's *The American Irish* does not appear to consider him. There appears to be neglect here, considering that the field is not so very crowded. On the other hand Larry McCaffrey, a thorough-going historian, provides trenchant comments on *Moon Gaffney* in his *Textures of Irish America* (1992). If I do not agree fully with McCaffrey, then maybe it is because I am less close to immigrant experience. I regard the provocations of *Moon Gaffney* as seminal and particularly constructive in the sociological context of the religious rigidity of Irish America. *Moon Gaffney* contains the repugnances always available in Irish-American fiction, but here directed at the excesses of a ruling class self-consciously forgetful of its immigrant origins. Sylvester's novel also is a vehicle for an updating of the effects of assimilation into American life.

I like the rhythm and flair of Sylvester's writing as well as the novel's anti-decorative message, which is protected from protesting too much by the clarity of Sylvester's portraiture. The energizing satire of the writing modifies, I think, the "frivolous" and "cruel" aspects of social relations in the novel that McCaffrey finds. There is a good deal in McCaffrey's comment on the courting rituals–"Alcohol is not a substitute for sex"–though there is a description of mature flirtation between Moon and Rosemary Danaher, whose father is also a commissioner.[4] Rosemary is a conservative socialite. The most sympathetic woman in the fiction, Ellen Doarn, holds her own against the toadying of her boyfriend Peter Calahan.

Ellen shines in the panaroma of the affluent, spiritually inert society around her, typifed by the two priests who try

---

4. Lawrence McCaffrey, *Textures of Irish America* (New York: Syracuse University Press, 1992), pp. 63, 73.

to talk her back into the broken engagement with Calahan. One of these is Father O'Driscoll who maliciously gives wrong advice about the rhythm method of birth control to girls at Mount Murphy. McCaffrey mentions him as representative of knavish priests in Irish-American fiction. In general, Sylvester's sketches of priests are less lugubrious than most others in Irish-American fiction, even if not as well crafted as those of J. F. Powers.

Sylvester's picture of the church is even-handed. Ellen goes to see Mount Murphy's Mother Thomas Moore for advice about resisting the clerical enforcement of her marriage. The reverend mother, who stands in for progressive Catholicism, disposes of Father O'Driscoll as if he were a wet tea rag: "We had him here for a while and since then he's been chaplain of an athletic club, a professional addresser of communion breakfasts and I don't know what else. I wonder he ever gets round to saying Mass" (*MG* 234) The strength of Sylvester's stance on the church is that it presents both sides of the coin—that which belongs to "The Hall," and that which belongs to the Gospels.

Mother Thomas Moore enacts the contemplative side of radical Catholicism, reflecting for instance on the structural flaws of women's colleges, "We have too many girls come to us for the wrong reasons as it is . . . I think we even teach sometimes for the wrong reasons . . ." (*MG* 20). The circle around Dorothy Day—Linford Thomas, Ed Galvin, and others—deals with practical problems of protesting, feeding, and housing in reaction to such events as evictions from the archdiocese's slum property. Allegories of good and evil are underlined amid the ward and office ramifications of Irish new world empire and new found new world Irish Church. Sylvester throws Dante's *Inferno* and Butler's *Lives of the Saints* into the cauldron of stellar upward mobility. It is plain that Dorothy Day, embattled by the legionnaires of formulaic religion, is the eminence presiding over this morality tale. And against Dorothy Day Sylvester enlists my own cousin, Eddie Reeves, not only as the "heavy," the Croesus, but also as the ultimately spurned fiancé of Ellen Doarn:

> "You don't suppose that Doarn girl's really engaged to that stuffed shirt?"
> "Why not?" Moon said cheerfully."If you had what he had, she'd be engaged to you, too."
> "What's that?"
> "About half the tea in China," Moon said.
> "Oh, come, come," Kavanagh said. "His folks own a grocery chain. That's all."
>
> -(*MG* 20)

Those stores had eight hundred branches before they were sold to Safeway at the period the novel was written. Two farmboy brothers from County Clare built them up. The child of one of them, Eddie's sibling Dan, went on to own the Cincinnati Reds and the Los Angeles Rams and suffer football's first strike from his coach George Allen. Their father, James, had other distinctions. He served on the committee of wealthy Irish Americans who gave Yeats an income in old age. He supplied the funds for Joseph Campbell's Fordham chair. And he showed my mother a first edition of *Ulysses*. Despite his shabby appearance in *Moon Gaffney*, James Reeves did the state of letters some service.

May Saint Dorothy Day pray for them.

CHARLES FANNING

∾

LODESTONE:
FOLLOWING THE EMLY SHRINE

On Sunday mornings, my mother would go to Mass at St. Catherine's in downtown Norwood on her own, leaving my father, my two-year-old brother Geoffrey, and me; I was four. Making things out of clay was one of our favorite activities. I recall that we began with whales, my father's inspiration: shaping hefty chunks of gray or brown clay, smoothing the flanks, sculpting out the mouth and tail, drilling the blowhole with a pencil as a finishing flourish: it just felt great. I began to move on to more ambitious modeling projects of my own, using packets of "plasticine" in bright primary colors from the five-and-ten store. When I went off to first grade at age five in September 1948, clay modeling became my ticket to extra notice and praise. At Christmastime, I brought in a freshly minted manger scene, with Mary, Joseph, and the Christ Child surrounded by animals in a shoe box tableau. My classmates were intrigued. More important, the teacher, Miss Cataldo—on whom all the boys had a crush—was impressed. She invited the second graders in to look, and my reputation as an artist was established.

My clay models of buildings, rooms, scenes from history and literature grew more and more elaborate as I got older. The highlights of my plasticine career included the

Parthenon to scale with Phidias' lost statue of Athena recovered and reinstalled inside, the Egyptian temple of Karnak, nine feet long and supported by columns decorated with hieroglyphics, and a two-storey medieval castle with twelve rooms, including an armory, throne room, and chapel, a banquet hall with food on the table, and exterior walls molded stone by stone. In sixth grade came my *pièce de résistance:* the Coliseum at Rome, which ended up on display in the children's room of the public library in Norwood. Mounted on a square of plywood, my coliseum was nearly a foot high and three feet in diameter. In a photograph I still have, I count twenty statue-crowned columns and more than three hundred separate figures.

In the end, these early art projects would dramatically expand my world. Recognizing artistic potential in my clay models, my sixth-grade teacher and first mentor, Mr. Francis Lambert, had gone out of his way to find me a scholarship to the weekly community classes for children at the Museum of Fine Arts in Boston, and so, from September 1954 to June 1955, I rode two busses and an MTA trolley from Norwood deep into the city to the imposing neoclassical pile on Huntington Avenue. I had been to Boston, but not often and never alone. Now, I found myself at the age of eleven embarked on the cultural and geographical adventure of my young life. Mr. Lambert took me in to enroll and showed me how to get there, but after that, I was on my own.

Lately, I have been writing a book about my childhood, which includes a chapter on that "trip to Bountiful." To jog my memory of the MFA in the 1950s, I paged through old issues of the *Bulletin of the Museum of Fine Arts*. Upon opening the bound volume for 1954, I was surprised to find on its title page the photograph of an extraordinary artifact. The caption read, "Emly Shrine—Anglo-Irish—Eighth Century."

I was amazed. I could not recall having seen it during my year of grace at the museum but, from my study of early Irish culture, I knew what I was looking at. The piece was a reliquary. Hung around the neck or over the shoulder by a leather strap, it would have held the relics—bits of bone or hair—of a Christian saint. The date made it very early, and thus, probably very rare. The Emly Shrine looked to be an Irish national treasure that had somehow left its country of origin and landed in Boston. How had this happened?

Two further considerations piqued my interest. First, the name "Emly" brought to mind my favorite entry in the *Irish Annals*, the medieval manuscript collections of dated events from early Irish history. *The Annals of Inisfallen* record an event of the year 947: "*Duilend do nim for altoir nImblecha Ibair ocus in t-én do labrad risna doenib, ocus inganta ile archena isin bliadainse*: A leaf [descended] from heaven upon the altar of Imlech Ibuir, and a bird spoke to the people; and many other marvels this year." I first read this in Kathleen Hughes's scholarly classic, *The Church in Early Irish Society*—it is a lovely passage, literally miraculous, and perfectly evocative of early Irish Christianity.

Tucked into the part of County Tipperary that juts westward into County Limerick, Imlech Ibuir—that is, Emly—was a powerful site in the medieval church. In his 1837 *Atlas of Ireland*, Samuel Lewis identified "this place, noticed under the name of 'Imlagh' by Ptolemy, as one of the three principal towns of Ireland," and "formerly an important city and the seat of a diocese. A monastery of canons regular was

founded here by St. Ailbhe, or Alibeus, who became its first
abbot, and dying in 527, was interred in the abbey. His suc-
cessors obtained many privileges for the inhabitants." *The
Annals* report that Emly was important enough strategically
to be burned or plundered at least fifteen times between 845
and 1177. The place was also touched by the legendary
Brian Boru, who took hostages from the monastery in 987
"as a guarantee of the banishment of robbers and lawless
people therefrom." In 1015, "Fiach, son of Dubchrón, was
treacherously killed by Carrán's son in the middle of Imlech
Ibuir," and the same year saw the "vacating" of the
monastery, "and the invasion of Lothra." There was also an
extraordinary act of violence by the church against the state
at Emly in 1032, when the monastic household murdered a
Munster prince: "Étrú Ua Conaing, royal heir of Mumu,
was killed while violating [the church of] Ailbhe."

From the caption in the *Bulletin*, I found it impossible to
determine whether the Emly Shrine actually came from
Imlech Ibuir. But it may have.

A second thing, going back to the clay models and
miniatures of my childhood, attracted me to this reliquary.
The Emly Shrine is a small object, a box measuring four
and three-sixteenths inches long, by one and eleven-sixteenth inches wide, by three and eleven-sixteenth inches
high. Carved from a single block of yew wood, it is shaped
like a house with a trapezoidal sloped roof, which is the box
lid. All the edges are framed with rounded moldings of
gilded bronze fastened with small nails. An intricate,
stepped pattern of silver lines covers the surface of the walls
and roof, spreading concentrically from a regularly spaced
series of silver squares, each of which frames a four-part leaf-
like design. These interwoven lines of silver are inlaid into
the yew wood. Fixed onto the surface are three large gold

circular medallions, which dominate the design. These are triangulated, with two on the side wall and one on the roof of the little house. Each gold circle contains four inner circles and each of these is punctuated by cloisonné-inset enamel blocks of alternating yellow and green organized in multiples of eight. All three medallions are blank in the center, but—given the overall complexity of the piece—they must have once held something wonderful. On each end of the roof's bronze ridgepole perches the head of a fantastic animal whose eye, snout, and mouth are marked out in yellow, green, and red (now faded to brown) cloisonné blocks. These heads exemplify the wild mix of Celtic and Christian design motifs that identify Irish art throughout its golden age of 600–800 a.d. The two heads point inward along the roof line toward, in the center, a tiny house with its own sloped roof that echoes the shape of the shrine itself. This second house is inlaid with a cloisonné grid of twelve yellow and green blocks. As a whole, the piece is breathtaking in its delicate, balanced interplay of colors, lines, and surfaces.

For reasons that were not entirely clear to me, I found myself fascinated by this object, and over the past decade I have immersed myself in its history both in Ireland and abroad. My subsequent research has confirmed that the Emly Shrine was indeed a rarity, and something of a mystery, as well. I have found only four references to the item in Irish archeological literature. The earliest appears in the 1878 volume *Christian Inscriptions in the Irish Language*, by the eminent antiquarian George Petrie. In describing reliquaries "of the form of the earliest type of church," which is also "that of the ark, handed down from time immemorial," Petrie declares that "the most remarkable examples of such shrines" include but three in Ireland, including "Lord Emly's shrine." I learned also that before it came to Boston, the shrine had been exhibited publicly only once—at the Great Exhibition of Art and Industry that was held in Dublin from May through October of 1853.

At that point, I realized I might actually have seen the Emly Shrine once, myself. To commemorate the American Bicentennial, the Irish government mounted a spectacular exhibition, *Treasures of Early Irish Art, 1500 B.C. to 1500 A.D.* that toured the United States in 1977 through May 1979. Its Boston showing had coincided with my first sabbatical, some of which I used to take a special course of weekly lectures at the MFA on early Irish art, culminating with a private pre-view of the exhibition. Virtually all of the greatest examples of Irish culture's flowering were on display: the Ardagh Chalice, the Tara Brooch, the Cross of Cong, the Clonmacnoise Crozier, and on and on, even the Books of Durrow and of Kells. At the time, the exhibition provoked lively debate over whether it was wise of the Irish government to allow the bedrock artifacts of its heritage out of the country; certainly, no comparable exhibition has happened since.

The exhibition catalog, which I kept, recorded that the exhibition had consisted of sixty-nine objects. All but one was on loan from either the National Museum of Ireland, Trinity College Dublin, or the Royal Irish Academy. That one piece was listed as item number 31. "Emly Shrine, County Limerick." That's how important it was.

———

The man who sold the shrine to the Boston Museum of Fine Arts was named John Monsell. How his family had come to own it can be understood in historical terms. The greatest disruption to the Irish church since the Viking raids of the late 700s accompanied the Protestant Reformation in the reign of Henry VIII when, by decree, most monasteries and churches were destroyed or shuttered and all chattels of value confiscated. In 1539 a legislative act ordered Henry's representatives "to investigate, inquire and search where within the said land of Ireland there were any notable images or relics to which the simple people of the said lord the king were wont to assemble superstitiously and as vagrants to walk and roam in pilgrimage, or else to lick, kiss or honour contrary to God's honour." Once gathered, these "divers profane images, pictures and relics" should be "taken into the hand of the lord the king and appraised; and also sold for the use of the lord the king." During the Reformation, many Catholic abbots became laicized or went over directly as prelates into the new Protestant Church of Ireland, and they often took ecclesiastical art objects along with them to their new digs. In addition, members of the recently validated Anglo-Irish Protestant nobility did a fair amount of plain stealing of artifacts. It is safe to assume that somewhere in this hurly-burly of shifting allegiances and fortunes, the Emly Shrine went missing from its original ecclesiastical home.

The Monsell family had come from London to County Limerick in 1612 as part of the first land-grabbing plantation of Ireland after the Battle of Kinsale. In 1690, they built a notable Big House at Tervoe, Clarina, outside the city of Limerick, and at some unknown point in their progress, they acquired the shrine. The Monsells reached their genealogical peak when the current patriarch, William, was created Baron Emly of Tervoe in January 1874. Born in 1812 and educated at Winchester and Oxford, William Monsell went on to an eventful public career—serving as an MP for County Limerick, under secretary of state for the colonies, postmaster-general, and vice chancellor of the Royal University of Ireland. It was William who lent the shrine to the Great Dublin Exhibition in 1853. After that, according to a

1922 essay by E. C. R. Armstrong, "this reliquary was formerly deposited with the Royal Irish Academy by its owner, Mr. William Monsell, of Tervoe, co. Limerick, afterwards Lord Emly," and then, "the shrine was returned to Mr. Monsell in 1872."

This, in itself, is strange. Once deposited in the RIA, very few artifacts were ever taken back by their owners. Armstrong also remarks that the RIA had a plaster cast made, and it is this cast that is pictured in his essay. At that point the track peters out. A footnote says simply that "Presumably the shrine is still at Tervoe. A letter to the present Lord Emly asking for information on the subject failed to elicit a reply." Tervoe House is only twenty miles northwest of the town of Emly, and the latest of the four archaeological references—Joseph Raftery's 1941 catalogue, *Christian Art in Ancient Ireland*—states that "the exact locality from which the shrine came is not known, but as it has been in the possession of the Monsell family of Tervoe, Co. Limerick, for some time it may be presumed to have belonged at least to the south of Ireland."

The Monsell peerage was short-lived. William's son Thomas was the second and last Baron Emly. He succeeded in 1894, but died in 1932 without leaving a male heir. Thomas Monsell's only child, Mary Olivia Augusta, married Edmond James de Poher de la Poer in 1881. Their son Edmond (1883-1964) became a commander in the Royal Navy. He took Monsell as an additional surname in accordance with his grandfather Thomas's will, and Tervoe House was deeded to him in 1935. According to Raftery's 1941 account, "Through the kind courtesy and generosity of Commander Edmond Monsell, R. N., the Shrine has been deposited in the National Museum."

This new beneficence was most likely a World War II precaution; at some postwar point, the Monsells again took the shrine back to Limerick. In 1948, Edmond made the house over to his son, born in 1916 and a career officer in the British Army, who bore the exceptional name John Humphrey Arnold de Poher de la Poer Monsell. John and his family lived at Tervoe for only three years. He moved out in 1951 and sold the Tervoe Estates to the Irish Land Commission. In 1953 he had the house demolished. In between, in the course of a general tidying-up of the family's property, John sold the Emly Shrine to the Boston Museum of Fine Arts in 1952.

A bulky folder on the Emly Shrine in the archives of the MFA provides some clues as to how this extraordinary purchase came about, and also suggests the controversial nature of the transaction. Bringing the Emly Shrine to Huntington Avenue was a high point in the career of the MFA's medieval curator, Georg Swarzenski, who had left Nazi Germany and the directorship of the Municipal Museums of Frankfurt in 1937 to take a position in Boston. With his son Hanns, affiliated with the Institute for Advanced Study in Princeton, Swarzenski built Boston's medieval collection virtually from scratch. Between them, the two men knew every important art collector and broker in Europe.

The intermediary between the Monsells of Tervoe and the MFA was Hector O'Connor of 77 Merrion Square, Dublin, a son of the well-known Irish-American sculptor Andrew O'Connor, who had lived out his last years in that house and died there in 1941. In a March 1952 letter to Hanns Swarzenski, Hector O'Connor declares himself "delighted to think that the Boston Museum is taking a serious interest in the shrine. It would be a great pity, I think, for them to miss such an important object. I took your advice and let the solicitor, Mr. Jackson, know that he may receive a communication from the Museum." The MFA file that I was shown contains no details of the ensuing negotiation.

The handwritten draft (a number of words are crossed out) of a reply from Hanns Swarzenski to O'Connor, dated November 6, 1952, indicates that the deal has been done:

My dear O'Connor,

This is just a note to tell you that the Shrine despite its small size has received the greatest admiration, and that we are all very happy that we have it here in our Museum. At your advice, we waited all these months before showing it to the Trustees, but now it will soon be exhibited and published in the Bulletin of the Museum by my father who wrote a beautiful scholarly paper about the piece and its connections with Irish and Anglo-Irish art. Needless to say how grateful I personally am to you and your adviser in procuring the shrine. I ~~only~~ hope indeed that nobody in Ireland will resent the purchase and that one will realize that to us this tiny object is the only representation and symbol of Irish art and culture we have in this country, while for you in Ireland it is but one of many examples of your great artistic heritage.

As I am told the Catholic Bishop of Boston unfortunately is not ~~very~~ really concerned with artistic matters and so we have not informed him of the purchase and asked him to write to the Papal Nuncio in Dublin to request a formal export license from the Minister of Education. You will remember that Mr. Jackson ~~and yourself~~ also thought it ~~better not to do~~ unnecessary to do this then and you agreed.

Clearly, the involved parties were aware of potential trouble; the hope that "nobody in Ireland will resent the purchase" is a telling aside. The Catholic bishop to whom Swarzenski referred was Richard J. Cushing, Boston's archbishop since 1944, who would become a cardinal in 1958. A man of great political acumen and strong opinions, Cushing was the son of immigrants from Galway to South Boston, where he had been born and raised. He remained intensely interested in the affairs of his parents' homeland; throughout the 1950s, for instance, he played a major role in financing the building of a new cathedral in the city of Galway, which he in fact personally dedicated in 1965. No one could have doubted that he would have had something to say about the MFA's plan to take the Emly Shrine out of Ireland.

But Ireland and Irish America, it seems, were not especially interesting to the MFA. A case in point is the essay by Georg Swarzenski announcing to the general public that the Emly Shrine had come to Boston, published in October 1954, two years after the purchase and his son's letter to Hector O'Connor. As with many pieces in the old MFA Bulletins, the institution's air of *noblesse oblige* and assumed cultural power leaps out to the reader.

Swarzenski's piece is a fascinating cultural document, and in some ways a precarious tightrope walk rife with contradictions. Its title is "An Early Anglo-Irish Portable Shrine"–a misnomer of which Swarzenski ought to have been aware. In the eighth century there was no "Anglo" in Irish society, and for that matter, very little "Anglo" in Britain. Swarzenski provides little detail on provenance, saying only that "the object . . . has been for centuries in the Monsel [sic] (Lord Emly) family in Limerick County." He provides no details about how the 1952 acquisition came about or how much money was spent, revealing only that the purchase (Accession Number 52.1396) came through the "Theodora Wilbour Fund in memory of Charlotte Beebe Wilbour." He is hugely enthusiastic about the shrine, averring that it is one of six surviving complete examples of "evidently analogous works," only one of which, the Lough

Erne Shrine, remains in Ireland, in the National Museum.
The mention of the National Museum leads to a preemptive
justification:

> There is a popular claim that such [rare] works, for
> their national interest involved, should be treasured
> alone in the representative collections of the native
> country which are, indeed, and always will be, the
> particular and unrivaled domain of the arts in this
> field. However, Anglo-Irish art of this period spread
> from the beginning over many countries, and the
> object shows how its national roots had grown to uni-
> versal human expression and were generally under-
> stood and adopted in scattered places of Western and
> Central Europe.

In other words, by virtue of its translatable excellence,
this art had been rendered no longer merely "Irish." "Only
a narrow-minded attitude," Swarzenski continues, "might
complain that [the shrine's] purchase, by the Museum of
Fine Arts, had deprived the native country of a documentary and sentimental national value."

Swarzenski's argument then takes another specious, and
palpably condescending, turn:

> On the contrary, the singular subject, accessible now
> among outstanding works of cosmopolitan rank, will
> display here the legitimate importance of this realm,
> and might, especially in Boston, as we hope, con-
> tribute to an awakening and deepening of the his-
> toric and artistic understanding of this city's Irish
> population.

Implying that such understanding is at present asleep and shallow, Swarzenski appears to be visualizing the great unwashed of South Boston, Charlestown, Brighton, Norwood, trooping into the MFA on weekends to be enlightened by exposure to the handiwork of their forebears.

The rest of the essay develops these two incompatible themes. On the one hand, he takes pains to refute the originality of early "Irish" art, references to which always appear in quotation marks. He claims that the famous treasures of manuscript illumination and metalwork, which I was to see at the MFA in 1978, mostly derive from continental and Near-Eastern models. He contends that "the figural representations in the *Book of Kells* are copies–the classical mind says caricatures–of a famous continental manuscript." And yet, Swarzenski is unable to restrain his enthusiasm for the distinctiveness of the Emly Shrine itself. He asserts that "the richer, more articulate development of the ridge pole . . . is unique for inventiveness and elaboration," and that the technique of cutting the rectangular step-pattern into the yew wood first, and then beating the silver lines into the surface appears on no other extant reliquaries, and is, in fact, "unparalleled in the Western schools of the period."

The shrine appears to have entered Boston with as little fanfare as it left Ireland. There was no significant coverage of the shrine's arrival in Boston in the local papers. In the MFA archive shown to me in 2001, the only contemporary response to the purchase of the shrine is a letter of October 21, 1954, from Alastair Martin, a noted New York medieval collector and donor to the Metropolitan Museum of Art, thanking Georg Swarzenski for sending him...

a copy of your very interesting and erudite article on the Emly Shrine. It is certainly a great rarity, and of

considerable historical and artistic importance. I hope
to see it soon. As you know, I made a desperate effort
to get it myself, and congratulate you on your success
in obtaining it. Should your museum ever come
across such a piece, and doesn't wish it, could you let
me know.

I have been able to find only one reference anywhere—a
brief mention in the *Boston Globe* weekly column, "Notes
of Irish Interest," for October 12, 1954, buried on page
twenty-four—announcing the purchase by the MFA "some
years ago" of the "Emly Limerick Shrine." The writer
quotes and paraphrases from Swarzenski's "interesting, if
somewhat technical, essay on early Irish art." If there ever
was a press release issued about the acquisition, I have not
been able to find one in the MFA file or elsewhere. It
appears that regardless of its importance, the museum was
not looking to draw attention to the acquisition.

But the reaction at the Royal Society of Antiquaries of
Ireland—headquartered at 63 Merrion Square, just a few
doors from the home of Emly intermediary Hector
O'Connor—was something else entirely. In his April 1955
annual address on "The Position of Irish Archaeology,"
Seán P. Ó Ríordáin, the society's president and the foremost
Irish archaeologist of his generation, cautioned that "very little advantage has been taken of the powers conferred by the
1930 [National Monuments] Act." In a section headed
"Export of Antiquities," Ó Ríordáin deplored the loss of the
shrine:

Apart from the safeguarding of monuments and the
reporting of finds, the 1930 Act gave power to pre-
vent the export of archaeological objects. I wish to

mention one sad instance of this export, which may be a salutary warning. I know nothing of the details but it was with a sense of shock that it was learned that the Emly Shrine, an important Early Christian reliquary, had left the country. The first public intimation that this had occurred was an article in an American journal. I do not know what were the preliminaries to the export of the shrine but I do know that the Irish public was also unaware of the situation and was therefore given no chance to enter the market for its purchase. One remembers with gratitude the cases in the nineteenth century when outstanding objects were saved by public subscriptions initiated by the Royal Irish Academy or its members.

If, in fact, any sort of storm followed this blistering reaction, the MFA weathered it and the Boston press did not cover it. In any case, Ó Ríordáin's indictment was not included in the MFA folder on the shrine. However, later documents collected there do illustrate a significant increase in respect within the art world for the piece over the ensuing years. The Emly Shrine has left the museum only twice since its arrival in 1952. During its two years of travel with Treasures of Early Irish Art, it was insured for $300,000. The shrine's second excursion was to an exhibition at the Palazzo Grassi in Venice in 1991; at that point, the MFA upped the insurance to $2.5 million.

The last tantalizing bit of the record in the mystery is an internal MFA memorandum of September 30, 1994, from a staffer reporting to his colleagues that "a Trina Vargo from the foreign policy division of Senator [Edward] Kennedy's office in Washington DC had called with regard to the interest of an Irish museum in the Emly Shrine. It was unclear whether this was a loan request or a repatriation overture." A follow-up call revealed that an official from the National Museum of Ireland had asked Senator Kennedy to help get the reliquary back. "They further indicated," the memo continues, "that the shrine had been in our collection for 60 years, that it was not displayed prominently, and that they would love to get it, since they had nothing like it." Furthermore, "There was no implicit or explicit implication that the object ought to be in Ireland, or ought not to be here." The memo concludes: "I explained to Ms. Vargo that we did not typically sell objects from our collection to other museums, and we were not interested in parting with the Emly shrine. She will indicate to the National Museum that we were pleased to hear from them, but that we are not interested in pursuing their proposal."

For me, the Emly Shrine has become something of a cathetic lodestone, one with great drawing power, and the fate of this object has come to overlap with my own lifelong engagement with Ireland and its culture. I see the shrine as a figure for the interests that have spurred my teaching and scholarship in Irish Studies. Within this field, I've sought to establish the existence of a body of literature—that of the Irish in America—that had been variously forgotten, misunderstood, and underappreciated; and to place that body of literature anew in clarifying cultural contexts. When I started out in the late 1960s, the entrenched Anglophile and Anglocentric predispositions in literary studies resisted such an effort. I recall job interviews, some in places now known as bastions of Irish Studies, where I was at pains to explain my interest in

Irish culture, much less Irish America. More than once, scholars who should have known better responded to my research by making lame jokes, along the lines of "Irish-American culture? You mean besides drinking?"

Just as a reliquary is, if understood in its context, much more than a container for dead bones, so is a literary tradition much more than antiquarianism. Similarly, I believe that the Emly Shrine was bought quietly and then buried out of context by Boston's Museum of Fine Arts. Yes, the powers at the MFA saw the shrine as valuable. But they could not acknowledge its importance as a work in the Irish tradition; the Swarzenski essay does not so much as admit there was an Irish tradition.

The Emly Shrine was a new treasure at the MFA in the mid-1950s, during the time I was a Saturday student there. Given the behind-the-scenes nature of the purchase negotiations, I cannot imagine that the shrine was displayed very prominently; I only know that I didn't notice it. However, I can easily verify the contention in the Kennedy memo that the piece has been kept at the margins in more recent years. When I visited the museum in 2001, the Emly Shrine was one of six or seven disparate pieces clustered on the bottom shelf of a small case hanging on the wall outside the main medieval gallery. All were identified only by numbers, and a typed list of the names beside the case explained that these works had come from "Roman Provinces." As the Romans had at most a negligible presence in Ireland—until recently, most scholars believed they never ventured across the Irish Sea—even this was patently untrue.

I returned again five years later to find the shrine moved to a much better spot, but still woefully out of context. It had been shifted to the Catalonian Chapel, a small room off the medieval gallery dominated by a curvilinear Catalan fresco, described as "among the greatest twelfth-century European paintings in the United States." The shrine is at the bottom center of a four-by-six-foot display case that hangs on a side wall and holds "Precious Objects for Sacred and Secular Use." There are twenty of these, including a "Eucharistic dove" from Limoges, an English marriage casket, a Spanish astrolabe, two Dutch medallions, the escutcheon of a Florentine wool-merchants guild, and very different types of reliquaries from Germany and France. Every piece in this mixed bag is late medieval—the earliest date is 1150; the latest, 1504—except for the Emly Shrine. The shrine is now included in the MFA's general audio tour, where a sonorous, British-accented voice explains that "only nine medieval Irish reliquaries of this early date in this shape are known to survive today," and adds that the name is "for the Emly family of County Limerick who owned it in the nineteenth and twentieth centuries."

The Emly Shrine looks lonely in the Catalonian Chapel. Out of time and out of place, it is 300 years older than anything else in the room, and the only Irish art object anywhere in sight. I think of its placelore connections with the perilous history of the early church in Ireland, of its shadowy provenance from Henry VIII to the Monsells of Tervoe to the Boston museum, of its rarity and stunning aesthetic qualities, which were on public view in its native country only once, in 1853. That this great work of art has survived so much and ended up where it is now seems to me an injustice; only one among myriad injustices in the museum trade, to be sure, but sharply poignant nonetheless. Nothing about the Boston setting of this miraculous survivor is commensurate with the Emly Shrine's capacity for wonder.

From Huntington Avenue, it's still a long way to Tipperary.

Misgivings

EAMONN WALL

∾

THE BLACK HILLS, THE GOREY ROAD

My children were asleep and my wife was inside reading on a bed, while I was sitting outside of our rental cabin in a campground a few miles outside of Custer, South Dakota. It was the longest day of the year and the evening was cloudless and cool, the sky enormous in one direction and blocked by pine trees in another. I was a long way from home, aware all day as I drove westward of the widening gap between where I was now and where I had left on my American journey, begun twelve years before when I had loaded suitcases into a car and headed for Dublin Airport.

But I was so happy: since childhood I had dreamed of driving across America but doubted if I'd ever get the opportunity to accomplish it. As kids, we referred to Custer the man as "General Custard," which made him familiar to us, and this was one silly thing which occurred to me this afternoon when we rolled into Custer, the town.

We had driven here from Omaha, where we live now, so we had not come far; however, each of us, in our own way, as the radio played a steady diet of Patsy Cline and Hank Williams, felt the impact of the miles, markers, and the steady rising movement toward the hills. The West had begun to become a presence we could feel. Somewhere west of Valentine we had crossed into a new and sacred territory. To a degree, I'd been prepared for this: two sentences from Kathleen Norris's *Dakota: A Spiritual Geography* had been running round and round in my head for a couple of weeks. The first went like this: "Nature, in Dakota, can indeed be an experience of the holy."[1] The second followed thus: "The sense of place is unavoidable in western Dakota, and maybe that's our gift to the world."[2] I suppose it was this book more than anything that had inspired my visit. I wished to view for myself this "holy" landscape, experience this "holiness" first-hand, and measure it against "the holy ground" of Ireland that I knew so well. Also, I wanted to drive to Dakota and witness "sense of place" in a topography I felt strangely drawn to, but for which I felt singularly unprepared. In Ireland, place, personality, and identity are inseparable; however, I doubted whether the Irish emotional lens I observed the world through—the narrow street, the small field, the wet grass —could accommodate these huge, dry vistas located in the center of the American continent.

In this frame of mind, I arrived. A few hours earlier, we had been delayed because the main road was blocked by construction. We took a secondary route and got blocked there too. A Native American woman directing traffic, with a stop/go sign, told me to drive back a few miles and turn onto a dirt road that would connect with the main road beyond where another crew were working, so I followed her directions—I went back, and turned left, and proceeded slowly up the winding dirt road, over the red earth of the Black Hills. It was an extraordinary, and quite accidental, experience—to be in the dark center of a forest

1. Kathleen Norris, *Dakota: A Spiritual Geography* (New York: Ticknor and Fields, 1993), p. 1.
2. Norris, p. 169.

in the middle of a continent, in a white station wagon with my wife and children. When we stopped the car, which we did frequently, I listened to the sound of the breeze blowing the low lying branches of the evergreens, and felt the cool air coming from the forest into the car and touching our mesmerized faces. Above the road was the brightness of a sky without clouds, and to each side the great darkness and mystery of the forest.

I remained quiet. I listened to the excited voices of my wife and children who were in awe of the opportunity to be present here that chance had presented. I knew too, because similar events in my own childhood had transfixed me, that my children were learning the language of the landscape of their country. My wife, as she watched and spoke, understood that she had come home to her people and to her own childhood: it was the trees that told her this. I felt the mystery, power, and gravitational pull of sacred ground. What seemed so important to me was the knowledge that my children were finding their places in their own landscape, as I had found mine in the County Wexford of my childhood.

Two years before, I had brought them out of New York City and placed them on the American prairie: it concerned me that I had stolen their sense of belonging to a place. I felt I had. But this morning I understood I'd delivered them to another. Instead of belonging to just one place—something which strongly afflicts me—they had now inherited a multiple sense of belonging and a healthy attitude to the world. I had brought them away from the superficial, in a sense, toward the center of place. Thomas Merton has described life as an inward journey: I understood that we had arrived at this inward place—the Black Hills—where we were meant to bury that oar. Here was a day, here were the parts

of a day, so important and unforgettable. For once, because
parenthood allowed me to be both observer and participant,
I was able to know history as it happened and not just as
memory. As a father, I have been taught by nature that my
own desires, my life in fact, is secondary to my children's;
therefore, I have been freed from self to become facilitator
and observer.

But it was also possible, perhaps even likely, that the
intensity experienced on that longest day in the Black Hills
represented a certain apex in my life as husband and parent. The feeling was one that mixed joy and sorrow: we
had reached a fork in the road at which we separated—
three going in one direction, myself in another, and it
seemed to me that I was about to begin the immigrant
experience all over again. By bringing them to the center
of their landscape, I was reminded of the distance separating me from my own. At the same time, I had given a wife,
a son, and a daughter the gift of the country they had been
born to. Were all of these—love, marriage, fatherhood—
mere coincidences or connected to fate? It seemed quite
wonderful to me that I, a stranger and an immigrant, was
the one who had guided my wife and children to the center of their native land. To be happy in the world, you
must feel that you have ventured out from some place
called home which has filled you with what we call sense
of place, and which has given you the confidence to continue with your travels. For them, the Black Hills was one
such starting point.

Suddenly, after rounding a corner, we found our way
blocked by a buffalo. My son told me that they are called
bison, that buffalo is incorrect. I couldn't believe how big it
was, how slowly it walked. I had been trained as a driver in
rural Ireland, so I was used to sharing the road with animals.

Still, this was a new experience and I wasn't sure how to react. If I drove up close behind the animal and honked the horn, would he run off into the forest, or would he rear up in anger and damage the car? In the Irish scenario, there would have been many animals—sheep or cattle—but also a farmer and his dog. In the end, we turned the car around to find the point where we had left the blacktop and joined the dirt road. We turned back because of what my fellow travellers had agreed upon: the buffalo owned the forest and the dirt road, so it was for us to yield, not him. A short while later, we passed the point where the woman had stood directing traffic and where the men had been working on the road. Not only had the crew departed, but there was no sign at all of the road even having been opened and new tarmac laid. It was as if this crew had been spirits sent to direct us to the dirt road, the forest, and the buffalo.

———————

America is a huge and complex country. As a child growing up in Ireland, I understood it to be simpler than Ireland. Now I know it would take many lifetimes to uncover its mysteries, beauties, and divisions. But, on that evening in the campground outside of Custer, I wasn't interested in working hard on those difficult issues. Instead, I sat in the pure peacefulness of evening full of the whooping joy of arrival—watching, breathing, opening up like a flower. On the road that morning, somewhere between Valentine and Chadron in the Nebraska Sandhills, I was reminded of another road—the one that connects my hometown of Enniscorthy, County Wexford, with the small seaside village of Courtown. My father is at the wheel of a Ford Cortina, which is full of children. This road and these names are a mantra for me framing my childhood. As I have driven other roads in cars or buses, or looked out the windows of trains, or sat alone in airports waiting to board a plane, I have often been reminded of the feelings of exultation sparked by the pulling away of the family car from the curb in Enniscorthy and the beginning of the brief, yet enormous and mythical, trip from town to seaside.

Each road I travel repeats, recalls, defines, refines, and returns me to that one road and that singular world of childhood. My mind wanders backward: I note the garages that frame one side of the Island Road, then St. Mary's Graveyard where my grandparents are buried; then the ditches alive with daisies, primroses, and wild fuchsia fighting for light through the briars; and the barley-rich fields of the "The Model County." On pasture land, cows graze quietly, or loll in the summer sun. I remember, on the old road through Blackstoops, the exact point where a table was set on which were placed strawberries and honeycombs for sale, and I remember once, in the back of the car, tearing into a comb with my fingers and teeth—like a bear in a cartoon—before passing it on to my brother for his turn. At Scarawalsh, the road divides: one way, the sea—the other, Bunclody and the mountains. Then Ferns, the ancient capital of Leinster and the seat of Diarmuid MacMurrough, who brought the Normans to Ireland. Along the wide stretch of road outside Ferns, near the Halal meat plant, are large banked fields full of sheep, and to the east, the railway line. Then Camolin, then the shopfronts of Gorey—McCormack's, the 64, French's, O'Connor's, Hurney's, Cooke's and Webb's—and the town full of Saturday shoppers. As we enter Courtown, we see,

to our right, the ballroom and, above us, the sea. We turn
right and, when the car stops, jump out and abandon our
father to the bags and boxes.

On that evening in South Dakota, my heart had slowed
and my will retreated. I had arrived. On another continent, I had recreated a journey made in childhood. I
looked across at the trees and tried to imagine what journeys my children would make when they were grown and
wondered what they might remember of our coming to
the Black Hills. What I lacked that night was a sense of history. As a child driving from Enniscorthy to Courtown, I
was crossing a landscape and a history that I felt I understood, if I didn't quite. Of the Black Hills I knew little.
Visually, all previous experiences had left me unprepared
for them. Of my knowledge of its history, I knew this: if I
examined it, I would be shown that almost everything I
had picked up previously was wrong.

Many afternoons, as children during the Christmas holidays, my friends and I showed up for the afternoon mati-
nee at the Astor Cinema in Enniscorthy. We were between
the ages of seven and ten, so it must have spanned the
years from 1962 to 1966. Most of us had no televisions at
home then; therefore, the cinema represented a vital out-
let, was an important contact with the outside world, and
was excitement personified. Two movies were shown each
afternoon: we went on days old westerns were shown. The
slick new releases, in which John Wayne appeared in
color, were shown at night, and were more expensive.
These movies represented my first visual contact with
America: whatever familiarity I developed with America
was gleaned from such movies or "pictures," as we used to
call them. I don't recall reading any books about America
during childhood; instead, I read about British war heroes

since these books were readily available, and fairly inexpensive, in the shops. I'm sure that the county library had plenty of books about America; however, I was unable to enter it, because I had failed to return a previously borrowed book and feared the wrath of the librarian. At that time, one didn't read Irish children's books, except in school, since none were available, at least not in the country. Until the middle of the 1970s, when newsagents expanded their stocks, it was difficult to buy books in rural Irish towns. As a result, despite the election, the Irish visit, and the assassination of President Kennedy, America was remote from me. I was the product of an Ireland that was rich, intense, and quite wonderful—except for primary school—but which was isolated. With the benefit of communication and Ireland's place in the international economic community, the generations who grew up in the 1970s and 1980s have a much greater sense of what is happening in America. They know America, or feel they do, whereas we hadn't a clue beyond what appeared on the movie screen. I can't recall ever meeting an American as a child, and I stayed away from television, which was dominated by American programs, since the medium didn't appeal to me.

We brought our cap guns and cowboy paraphernalia with us to the Astor Cinema. Quickly, we identified who the enemy was in the movie and started blasting away. The cacophony in the cinema was beyond belief: a couple of hundred guns shooting and plenty of shouting, and stomping of feet. This was an innocent time in Ireland—before the "Troubles" resumed in the North. But I remember growing out of this sort of entertainment—at the age of ten or so—when someone got the board game Risk for Christmas, and when our gang learned how to play bridge. But it remained true and unaltered that the first visual sight of America to fill my imagination was provided by Hollywood. At times, in high excitement, the River Slaney became the Rio Grande and the Bare Meadows the desert. The Cowboys and Indians were cartoon characters; the former were generally the "good guys"–they looked like us and were Christians–and the latter the "bad"–they looked and acted like heathens. Clearly, these movies were underlined by a not-too-subtle racism, which I didn't notice at the time as I was either too young or naive or both. Later on, I developed and have maintained a deep interest in American writing and music: it was these, I believe, which brought me to America.

———

The Black Hills were formed "in the Pleistocene upheaval that brought forth the Rockies. . . and [form] a remote ridge of granite and limestone—one hundred miles by forty—soaring over the surrounding landscape, basking in their peculiar isolation, and commanding a vast arc of the plain below."[3] For centuries, these mountains and surrounding lands had been the home to the Kiowa, Hidatsas, and the Mandan. These tribes were supplanted by the Sioux who had crossed the Missouri River in search of a new homeland after being hounded out of their own lands by the Chippewa, their hereditary enemy, in what became Minnesota. The Chippewa, who lived to the east of the Sioux and closer to areas the white men inhabited, got hold of guns from the Europeans, which resulted in their supremacy over the Sioux. Eventually, the Sioux were armed with guns and this, in tandem with their adept use of horses, made them the dominant power in their new homelands, which included much of modern-day North

3. Edward Lazarus, *Black Hills/White Justice* (New York: HarperCollins, 1991), p. 3.

Dakota, South Dakota, Iowa, and Nebraska. While in Minnesota, the Sioux were settled but, with the move westward, they followed the buffalo in spring and summer and camped during the late fall and winter months. The Sioux who inhabited the Black Hills were the Tetons comprising the Oglala, Brule, Hunkpapa, Miniconjous, Sans Arc, Two Kettle, and Blackfeet.[4] But we must be careful with these names: clearly, many of them are French, and it would be more proper, for example, to use Sicangu instead of Brule. In his book *In the Spirit of Crazy Horse*, Peter Matthiessen quotes John Fire Lame Deer:

> Our people don't call themselves Sioux or Dakota. That's white man talk. We call ourselves Ikce Wicasa–the natural humans, the free, wild, common people. I am pleased to be called that.[5]

One cannot overestimate the importance of the these Black Hills to the Sioux. Although they have inhabited them for a comparatively short period of time, the hills have, nevertheless, become the physical and spiritual promised land to which the Sioux have been delivered. At the top of a flyer for Mel Lawrence's film *Paha Sapa*–the title is "Black Hills" in the Lakota language–the following statement appears:

> The Black Hills of South Dakota are to the Lakota Sioux and Cheyenne Indians what Mount Sinai is to the Jews, the Vatican is to the Roman Catholics, and Mecca is to the Muslims. Sacred to the Indian–but not to the white man–the Black Hills have come to symbolize the misappropriation of Indian lands by the U.S. government.[6]

4. Lazarus, p. 4.
5. Peter Matthiessen, *In the Spirit of Crazy Horse* (New York: Viking, 1991), p. xxv.
6. "Native Peoples," Fourth World Documentation Project (http://fttp.gdn.org/fwdp/Resolutions/Tribal/lakota74.txt.), p. 1.

The great Hunkpapa Sioux chieftain Sitting Bull declared that "God made me an Indian and put me here, *in this place.*"[7] The hills are the home to Wakan Tanka, the Great Spirit, and "according to tribal legend these hills were a reclining female figure from whose breasts flowed life-giving forces and to them the [Teton] went as a child to its mother's arms."[8]

When I read the history books and learned of the level of injustice inflicted then and now on the native people by the United States, I forgot, for a while, all about the spiritual power of the Black Hills. I read that the great leaders Crazy Horse and Sitting Bull, who had defeated Custer at the Battle of the Little Big Horn on June 25, 1876, were both murdered, years later, after surrendering to the United States; that Big Foot and his followers were massacred at Wounded Knee by the United States, after they had handed over their weapons, on December 29, 1890; that Indian children were forcibly educated to ensure that they would lose their own language and culture; that religious rites, such as the Ghost Dance, were proscribed; and that lands were taken away "in exchange" for reservations. I read of dire poverty, lack of adequate health care, and of the general air of hopelessness which pervades Pine Ridge Reservation, where Wounded Knee is located, in South Dakota. I read the accounts of the occupation of Wounded Knee by American Indian Movement in 1973, which pitted a small armed group of Indian activists, led by Russell Means and Dennis Banks, against the firepower and resources of the United States; and the arrest, trial, and incarceration of Leonard Peltier for a crime that remains unproven.

Why do I find these accounts so shocking and disturbing? Certainly they undermine the view of America presented by

7. Elizabeth Cook-Lynn, *Why I Can't Read Wallace Stegner and Other Essays* (Madison: University of Wisconsin Press, 1996), p. 88.
8. Lazarus, p. 8.

the movies I saw in the Astor Cinema in Enniscorthy as a child, but I had a long time ago learned that that vision was false, that Hollywood presented the West as a cartoon with "real people." No, it's more than this. As an adult, I had built up an idea of the romance of America–generated by books, music, and the imagination–which was generally positive.

In itself, within its own borders, the United States represented an idea and a movement toward a benign resolution of its difficulties: there was a feeling that things would be worked out. My visit to the Black Hills has not only forced me to examine the concerted attempts by the United States to exterminate the Indians, but it has also made me think again of slavery; of the Civil Rights Movement; of the assassinations of Dr. King, the Kennedys, Lincoln, John Lennon; of the Vietnam War; of the Rodney King trial, and question my earlier assumptions. I am reminded of the limitations of my own reading and experience, and of how important it is to leave the library or office, venture out into the country or on to the streets, and ask such hard questions as: what are the impulses which have made America what she, he, or it is–the common good, racism, or what? But America, you know, is so seductive.

The other evening, I sat outside on the steps for an hour or so watching a few kids ride their bikes up and down our street. I heard their joyful cries and their screeching brakes. Earlier in the day, it had rained so heavily and powerfully–with accompanying thunder, lightning, and tornado warnings to the north–that now both the peace and the peculiar late orange light were overwhelming. I looked at the high silver maples, the well-kept lawns, and the long, straight, endless American footpaths I have come to like so much, and wanted to be frozen in this spot forever. It's easy to separate the personal from the political and the historical. In this instance, one of the children is mine: he has just learned how to ride a bike and I am sitting on a step watching him. Yet, my Irish childhood confirmed that for us–Irish people–such separations are impossible. In America, on the other hand, where progress and reinvention are pursued with such vigor, history is effectively filed and shelved like the old checks returned by the bank.

At the root of much of the trouble in the Black Hills is the second Fort Laramie Treaty of 1868, signed between the Lakota nation and the United States, "which recognized Lakota sovereignty in their Dakota-Wyoming homelands and hunting grounds, including the sacred Paha Sapa, the Black Hills."[9] In 1873, after gold was discovered in the Black Hills, the United States broke the treaty by illegally annexing much of the lands that fell under the aegis of the Fort Laramie Treaty and began the process of confining the Lakota to shrinking reservations on the poorest land. After a battery of legal challenges, the United States Supreme Court, in a landmark judgment, ruled in favor of the Lakota. At the conclusion of the longest running claim in American legal history, the Lakota were awarded more than $106 million in compensation and interest for the loss of the Black Hills. The court announced this decision on June 30, 1980, fifty-seven years after Ralph Case had filed the Black Hills claim.[10] In the end, after much debate, the Lakota rejected the settlement. As Edward Lazarus points out the monetary award was not as large as it appeared: if it were distributed on a per capita basis, each claimant would have received $1,500. Nevertheless, it surprised many that the inhabitants of some of the poorest areas in the United States were willing to reject such a large sum of money.

9. Matthiessen, p. xx.
10. Lazarus, p. 401.

However, the settlement was eventually rejected for reasons which had nothing to do with money:

> "I cannot accept money for the Black Hills," Severt Young Bear, a young activist, explained, "because land is sacred to me. . . . [The whites] are trying to change our value system. To be a traditional person is to believe in your own culture, is to believe in yourself as a Lakota person; then you cannot sell the land."[11]

Over time, some Lakota have felt that the settlement should have been accepted and the money invested in worthwhile enterprises. Maria Cudmore, the Cheyenne River Treasurer, believed that "with the world situation being what it is today, it would be futile to think we would ever get the Black Hills back."[12] To this day, the settlement monies are lodged in a bank and continue to earn interest while the United States Supreme Court has refused to hear motions that call for the return of the Black Hills to the Lakota with compensation for such resources as gold and uranium which has been extracted from the land.

————————

One factor that excited me the most about leaving Ireland for America was that my new home offered the possibility of *escape* from history. Certainly, to have grown up in the midst of ruins and old battlefields was exciting and a spur to the imagination. I grew up with the sense that my home area was important in both Irish and European history. When I read history as a child, or listened to a teacher recite it like a poem in school, I listened carefully. Eventually, despite going on to study it in college, I grew

11. Lazarus, p. 405.
12. Lazarus, p. 405.

disillusioned with it. History, I had begun to think, cluttered the landscape and cast a smokescreen over Irish life that hid other important, and less "heroic" aspects of Ireland. What was the point of history, I wondered, if all it did was induce hatred and leave children of the North without fathers or mothers? In America, I thought, I would be outside history and without a care. America, from my vantage point in Ireland, was new and not burdened by a lot of monuments to battle sites, monastic ruins, and the like. Also, I had now the opportunity to live in a country as an outsider, to not belong if I chose. I didn't feel I had to care. I had no voting rights. But what landscapes and the humans and animals that people then do is draw you into history: that hill over there, after all, has a name and a story to be told. Wherever I go, I am drawn toward the human voice. I am a good listener. When I traveled to the Black Hills, I was drawn into history. There was nothing I could do about it, and I felt the landscape invited me: first to listen, then to read, and finally to speak.

However, it is not easy to speak because, inevitably, I will be tempted to explore the common ground between the experience of the Irish and the Lakota. It is easy to be drawn into fallacy, to feel, as it were, that because one has lived one life, one understands another. Yet, certain issues— of land, language, identity, religion, culture—make our histories comparable. Also, such terms as "genocide" and "colonization" can be used in discussions of both. What makes me reluctant to draw conclusions are the writings of two Native American poets, Elizabeth Cook-Lynn and Wendy Rose, and scenes from *Rattle and Hum*, the documentary movie of a U2 tour.

After watching U2 perform "I Still Haven't Found What I'm Looking For" with a Harlem choir, I was angry: I felt

U2 was using the singers and the neighborhood to make the song seem more authentic, to suggest that the experiences of Irish rock stars and the people of Harlem were the same.[13] What right had U2 to make such assumptions? None in my book. But they had the money to pay the singers, to buy authenticity. A result of this, of course, was that the movie was so widely disseminated that many viewers left the cinema thinking that they had encountered truth. However, on another level, I understood that U2 were traveling to the source of music to pay homage to its roots, to show, in their duet with B.B. King, and in their performance of Bob Dylan's "All Along the Watchtower," how deeply Irish lives had been molded by these profound voices. Bridges between Ireland and America, they were reminding us, allow for traffic to move in both directions; however, we must tread modestly and carefully.

Wendy Rose finds that white American artists, in the general sense, have used Native American art in similar ways. She quotes the Lakota scholar Vine Deloria, Jr., who wrote that

> the realities of Indian belief and existence have become so misunderstood and distorted at this point that when a real Indian stands up and speaks the truth at any given moment, he or she is not only unlikely to be believed, but will probably be contradicted and "corrected" by the citation of some non-Indian and totally inaccurate "expert."[14]

Likewise, when underprepared yet well-intentioned American "experts" discuss Ireland, I am struck by the fact that such speakers do not believe Ireland to be a culturally

13. U2, *Rattle and Hum* (Paramount, 1988).
14. Wendy Rose, "The Great Pretenders: Further Reflections on Whiteshamanism," *The State of Native America: Genocide, Colonization and Resistance*, ed. M. Annette Jaimes (Boston: South End Press, 1991), p. 404.

separate entity but, rather, see it as an extension of the
United States. These experts, who give Irish Studies a bad
name, have learned the rudiments of deconstruction, post-
colonialism, and so on, in seminar rooms and feel well-
equipped to understand everywhere because, in their view,
one place is pretty much the same as the next: Pine Ridge,
the Bogside, Soweto, Kinshasa are all interchangeable.
Keeping this in mind, I asked myself: why should I raise
my voice on the subject of the Black Hills? It's certainly not
needed. Too many whites have misunderstood Native
American literature; why should I add my name to the list?

Like Wendy Rose, and the other Native American
writers I have read since my visit to the Black Hills, Elizabeth Cook-Lynn writes a straightforward and angry narrative. Her stridency reinforces in my mind the weakness of
theory and the distance that separates the seminar room
from the field. For Cook-Lynn—a member of the Crow
Creek Sioux Tribe, a poet, and an activist—it is neither
desirable nor practicable to be objective. It is her belief
that white people and their institutional centers of learning have poached from Native American culture and
homogenized it into "symbols and metaphors which are
developed in contemporary literary terms and in foreign
places outside of our traditional languages and lifeways to
describe who we are and where we have been."[15] A result
of this is that "indigenous peoples are no longer in charge
of what is imagined about them, and this means that they
can no longer freely imagine themselves as they once
were and as they might become."[16] In other words, if you
want to learn about Native American literature and life,
you should consult a white "expert" at your local college
campus who will locate both within cosmopolitan theoret-
ical constructs. According to Cook-Lynn, these scholars

15. Cook-Lynn, pp. 142–3.
16. Cook-Lynn, p. 143.

are more interested in relating Native American writing to the international scene than they are in studying Native America itself. Therefore, being Native American is neither credible nor important.

Cook-Lynn also claims that "Euro-American scholars have always been willing to forego discussion concerning the connection between literary voice and geography and what that means to Indian nationhood."[17] No critic of Irish writing can afford to ignore the connection between voice and place. Irish writers are collectively obsessed with place and in this respect, despite the effects of Christianity on Ireland, have much in common with Native American writers. The place which the Irish are drawn to combines the general and the particular: for example, the idea of home but also the memory of a singular fuchsia bush in a corner of a field or garden. In Irish writing–from the Old Irish nature poetry to the work of Seamus Heaney–there is a strong connection between people and nature, in its broadest sense. In his biography of Samuel Beckett, James Knowlson describes the Beckett family's holidays in Greystones, County Wicklow, and how deeply those ordinary days, and Greystones, influenced him as an artist:

> At night, the children could hear the waves crashing against the rocks and, through the windows overlooking the harbour, see the light of the Bailey Lighthouse near Howth flashing across Dublin Bay. These sights and sounds, together with those from Foxrock, Dun Laoghaire, and the Forty-Foot, were to stay deeply etched in Beckett's memory. He always loved the Irish countryside and its mountains. The County Dublin coastline with its lighthouses, harbours, viaduct, and islands permeated his

17. Cook-Lynn, p. 89.

imagination and pervaded his work. The recurrent images were, to use his own word, "obsessional."[18]

Although Beckett did not "name" place to the extent that many other Irish writers have done, the places of his childhood were located near, or at, the source of his creative flow. One can more readily feel and hear Ireland in Beckett than one can see it. For contrast, in Eavan Boland's memoir *Object Lessons*, we are confronted with the moment of separation from place, which is as powerful in Boland's life, if not more so, as the moment of engagement with it is for Beckett:

> One morning I was woken before dawn, dressed in a pink cardigan and skirt, put in a car, taken to an airport. I was five. My mother was with me. The light of the control tower at Collinstown Airport—it would become Dublin Airport—came through the autumn darkness. I was sick on the plane, suddenly and neatly, into the paper bag provided for the purpose.[19]

Boland was removed from Ireland, from her Irish childhood, from her feeling of belonging to a place, from the informality of youth, and removed to the Irish embassy in London, and later to New York, because her father was a diplomat. What Boland makes clear in her memoir is the negative effect that the forced termination of an Irish childhood had on her sense of identity as a person. The triumph of *Object Lessons* is the tale of how identity is rebuilt and how synonymous this is with her

18. James Knowlson, *Damned to Fame: The Life of Samuel Beckett* (New York: Simon and Schuster, 1996), p. 46.
19. Eavan Boland, *Object Lessons: The Life of the Woman and the Poet in Our Time* (New York: Norton, 1995), p. 35.

return to Ireland as a young woman. Perhaps ironically, she regains place and belonging in suburbia. A woman, poet, and mother, Boland was unwelcome in a male-dominated literary city that could not admit such a combination of activities. By travelling outward from the center of the city to the frontier of Dundrum, which was an unfinished suburb when she moved in, Boland established her own center and started a revolution in Irish writing. Hers was an inward move—physically and spiritually—which allowed her to recapture her place. The suburb, too, was a good place to live as it was here the "hand-to-mouth compromises between town and country" were most plainly evident.[20]

Boland's accounts of her childhood outside of Ireland, revealed in both her poetry and essays, have been of tremendous interest to me. All emigrés, exiles, and dislocated people are confronted by the distance between where they are now and the place of childhood. We must, like Boland, fill the void. In my life, I have not found this sense of place that Boland so eloquently describes perhaps because, unlike her, I have not returned to the country of my childhood, or I have remained closed to the possibility of belonging to America out of a kind of perverse loyalty to the place where I grew up. It is likely that I have adopted the attitude of the Irish emigrant for whom no place on earth can equal the locus of childhood. In fact, what defines Irish attachment to place so well is absence: one finds in Boland's work the plaintive voice of the exile mourning the separation from Ireland. What is ironic, of course, is the difference between yearning and fact. Although I have felt as Boland has, I have also been reminded on returning to Ireland why I was happy to leave when I did.

---

20. Boland, p. 169.

As I read Boland's memoir, I cast glances backward to
the Black Hills, and to the moments in the forest when our
path was blocked by the buffalo. What our journeys have
in common are children, and this binds us to Cook-Lynn
as well. What's surprised me about parenthood and made
it so remarkable is the fact that, for much of the time, I
have been the student and my children the teachers. From
their activities, I have learned:

> Is there something about the repeated action—about
> lifting a child, clearing a dish, watching the seasons
> return to a tree and depart from a vista—which
> reveals a deeper meaning to existence and heals
> some of the worst abrasions of time? [21]

In their midst in the Black Hills I felt the dark clouds
fade and the sun warm my tightened shoulders. I was following in my children's footsteps, and learning about
America from them. My body, the place I carry around
with me, was energized by the journey across the plains of
America. That simple journey—a family road trip—followed
by Boland's book has affirmed for me the certainty that
the acts of greatest significance in our lives are those we do
for others, for these return the greatest rewards. On the
longest day of the year, in the sacred Black Hills, these
truths were revealed to me.

The Lakota belief that the Black Hills is the source of
life reminds me of Seamus Heaney's work. In recent times,
and more than any other Irish writer, Heaney has
explored the deep connections between human beings and
the earth. For Heaney, the omphalos, or navel, or "the
stone that marked the centre of the world," connects both
the mother and child with the earth.[22] In Heaney's private

21. Boland, p. 169.
22. Seamus Heaney, *Preoccupations: Selected Prose 1968–1978* (New York: Farrar, Straus
and Giroux, 1980), p. 17.

myth, it is the water pump that joins people to the earth and sustains them physically and spiritually. The path from the human to the omphalos is also the path to the imagination. When people are removed from their sacred grounds, or when these grounds are appropriated by outsiders, the consequences are deeply felt. It is not merely a question of economics and deeds, it is much more than this: remove the Lakota from the Black Hills or the Irish from their wet fields, and you cut them off from the spiritual center that grounds them, gives them identity, and provides them with the temporal and spiritual waters, as Heaney illustrates. When the connection between place and person is violated or broken, life loses its meaning. The poet Wendy Rose notes that in her Hopi culture "the very worst punishment indigenous societies can inflict, much worse than death or imprisonment, is exile or to be stigmatized by your people."[23] How deeply these words resonate in the Irish psyche.

To return to Beckett. As a young man, he was a keen golfer and Knowlson reveals how the landscape and vista of Carrickmines Golf Club in Dublin remained with the writer throughout his life, in a quite surprising and magical way:

> Golf was for him, he told Lawrence Harvey, "all mixed up with the imagination," with the impact on him of the ocean, which one could see from the local course, and the landscape of the Dublin foothills. He knew, he said, "every blade of grass." At night, when he could not sleep, even many years later in France, he would play over and over again in his mind all the holes on the pretty bracken and heather course.[24]

23. Rose, p. 411.
24. Knowlson, p. 75.

To help himself fall asleep, Beckett recalled the repeated actions of the round of golf and their singular rhythms which also functioned as entry ways to the hills and the bay. Beckett brought himself back to place. Unlike Boland and Heaney, he seemed to resist place; in fact, he did no such thing.

I have resisted the Black Hills. Today, it's a tourist trap where you can see Mt. Rushmore, and Crazy Horse taking shape–and where you can gamble your money away in Deadwood. For many, the Black Hills mean Mt. Rushmore's triumphant faces. I have resisted out a fear of over-simplification, that I would make the all-too-easy connections between Irish history and Sioux history, between the battle at Wounded Knee and the battle of Vinegar Hill. It is true that they overlap; however, they are not the same. Also, I have resisted because I do not know the history of the Black Hills well enough, and because I am unable to speak the language. Nevertheless, I did travel to the Black Hills from Nebraska and I was a witness to their power and sacred qualities. The spirits of the hills overpowered my senses and I emerged from their corners transformed. Of this family roadtrip, of sense of place, of exile, of the brilliance of Eavan Boland's vision, of the longest day, I have borne witness.

ELIZABETH CREELY

∾

DAIRE NUA:
THE NEW OAK GROVE

There is a kind of acquired memory that gets formed from family artifacts—objects acquired accidentally or gained by inheritance—and from the small stories they contain. Things like a picture of a woman with a ridiculous hat. A gold ring that could never fit on any present-day finger, with an inscription attesting to eternal love. A rusty horse bridle with a large silver "C" engraved on it that hung in my grandfather's garage for years. (It now hangs on a wall in my apartment.) Most family artifacts come with a story, or with the hint of a story: I've always looked at the bridle and wondered what the name of the horse was that it was used to control.

These stories can feel like memory, embodied, experienced. They can feel like something you lived. False memory may shape you, just as surely as the geography of the place you live in shapes you.

But only if there is a story. What if there isn't one?

Stories can be hard to come by if one country was left for another because of disaster: war, for example, or in the case of my family, famine. If no one had stories of "home" to tell, or brought anything with them—and who had that luxury, amidst the stress and panic of something not quite deportation, but, well, very like deportation? If the people who left Ireland lived through a fear so intense that the conscious mind was ordered to face forward, it's likely that their living story was set aside and left behind, as something wholly unsuitable for the future. Why bring disaster with you?

In that sad and common case, the descendants of the emigrant will usually follow the example set for them: to never look back and never make any inquiry of what life was like, back then in those catastrophic and eventful times. They gathered their families together and ran.

This is the unspoken rule of the immigrant: don't look back while walking in uncertain terrain. And, while moving forward, don't engage in unreality. The immigrant Civil War soldier in the nineteenth-century song may wish he were in "dear old Dublin." But he knows that Dublin could not provide for him, could not accommodate his existence. He had to leave. What he remembers and longs for is not real.

I know much more about the Creelys than anyone else in my family, although I don't know much. I have casually researched the family name in Ireland (more than the actual family), using the usual lunch-hour search on Ancestry.com, an astonishingly easy and pleasingly quick method. Cobbled together from the research a cousin undertook twenty years ago, these researches have resulted in an incomplete profile of a family set in motion from Armagh to San Francisco by the combined forces of colonialism, disaster, and personal ambition.

But that's it: just big picture, impersonal stuff. Statistics, instead of story. No documentation. No letters, no photos. Just impenetrable silence, so typical of refugees. My great-great-great-grandfather, Patrick Creely, arrived in San

Francisco in 1851, near the height of famine-induced immigration in America. To be something other than a man in flight would make him a statistical anomaly. If he had been that rare Irish Catholic who came to America in the mid-eighteenth century, untroubled and confident, I don't believe he would have kept his mouth shut so tightly.

Patrick did not talk. He passed on his silence intact and it became the inheritance. I imagine when he lived, one would have needed a crowbar to pry open his mouth . . . and even then, what might have emerged would have been a shadow, a void in which the enlightening words swirled around like dry leaves.

The Creelys became "real," traceable through a paper trail of wills, death notices, directory advertisements, in California starting in 1875. Their residences and businesses—a blacksmith shop on Folsom Street, a house on Shotwell—are listed in San Francisco city directories. There is a picture of Edward Creely's veterinary hospital in San Francisco at Golden Gate and Polk streets, intact just two months after the 1906 earthquake. There are pictures of family members confidently riding horses, at ease in a landscape that did not threaten them with scarcity. All real.

We choose from these stories carefully. Some have been edited out of the family telling as too indicative of family failings: alcohol abuse, cars crashing into gas stations, the horse in Healdsburg, California, that broke my grandfather's hip, laming him for life. His brother James slapped its flank and startled it.

(Was the horse wearing the elaborate silver bridle? Is that why my grandfather saved it?)

My own memories were acquired under the influence of California: its coastal hills, fragile riparian environments, tidal zones, the foundation of granite that shifts and moves and is visible as the magnificent Sierra batholith. The Creelys have variously abused and admired, bought cheaply and sold dear, the land of California. Early on, we associated in halls and in churches, but at some point we left these institutions behind and ventured outside into "nature": the backyard, the large field across the street, the nearby Santa Ana Mountains. We met there. Habit, rather than memory, was the medium through which old ideas, old words, and old images flowed, the mute conveyer of custom. We lived at ease and in relative confidence—free, we believed, from famine and the indifference of a colonial government, free from the predations of nature.

I grew up walking in the great green, but even then, rapidly vanishing wild areas of Newport Beach, and Costa Mesa, both smallish towns in Southern California at the time. My dad, Christopher Creely, loved trees, rocks, and anything that was made by the combined forces of chlorophyll, geologic time, and weather. He walked his children everywhere, and while it was ostensibly for our health, I think his love of walking was also an atavistic urge descending on him, asking him to conduct a survey of the land he lived in.

Consider what is real, Christopher, something urged him. Look at the earth. Look at the sky. These things are real and constant. They don't change. Stay with the project: keep making discoveries about this place called California. Learn it by heart. (Did his great-great-grandfather Patrick Creely look at the coastal hills, and compare them with the drumlins of northeastern Ireland? When he looked at the San Francisco Bay, or the wetlands of the California Delta, what did he see? What did he compare these vast bodies of water to? How long did he rely on comparison in order to understand where he was?)

Christopher Creely and his five children walked on terrain that was under constant threat from real estate developers, who were displacing California's native flora and fauna—the gnatcatcher, mountain lion, condor, and other species too numerous to list—and replacing them with houses that sprang up on the freshly graded hills. The water that was requisitioned from California's rivers brought artificially bright lawns and non-native species to Southern California, with ecologically disastrous results—castor bean, pampas grass, ice plant, and hundreds more invasive species gone wild.

The first landscape I remember my dad taking me to, when I was four and he was about forty-two, was Upper Newport Bay or the "Back Bay," so called because of its location due east of the Newport Beach coastline. It's a tidal estuary, odiferous and a bit slovenly, full of rich black mudflats. It smelled hellish. Like many estuarine environments in Southern California, it was situated near an expensive housing development, built to take full advantage of the ocean view to the west, all the while polluting the watery mud at its feet with gray water runoff. Nitrogenous pollution from the nearby Irvine Ranch covered the waters of the estuary with a mat of bright green algae.

There were fish that swam in the estuary, mythological creatures who couldn't be seen, but whose presence I felt as a swarming energy. If I got too close to the mudflats and the water, my dad would grab me back, guarding me from the things in the murky bay: small sharks and stingrays. The place was uncanny and impossibly green. It surged with the full force of life. It was not benevolent and not malicious, but was solely concerned with its perpetuation: endangered and dangerous in equal measure.

(Years later, I would dream of stepping carefully across stepping-stones that paved a wide waterway filled with murky water: it was oil slicked and iridescent. The shapes of unfamiliar fish swam below its surface. *Come away, O human child*, To the water, the wild shapes called to me. In my dream, I ran from them.)

In the estuary I sensed, rather than saw, the churning intertidal system pursuing its own ends; in with the new and out with the old. The bay shivered and swayed in response to the pull of the ocean. I was a mote in its wild eye.

Once the grasping mud stole my shoe, my precious shoe. In spite of my best efforts, I stepped carelessly, and was suddenly treading slime, terrifyingly liquid, with nothing solid underfoot. I fell and continued to fall. Dad stepped over to me and with a great yank got me to my feet and onto dry ground. His foot accidentally stepped on my hand, which was buried in the muck. I watched the mud collect around my shoe, holding it for a moment as if it were inspecting a curious artifact. Clear water bubbled up around the shoe, which was framed in black. Then it sank slowly and disappeared.

I began to cry. I told dad that I understood that he had stepped on my hand as punishment for losing my shoe (I knew that shoes cost money). He had green eyes that intensified when the sun hit them or when he was moved by emotion. At that moment, they glowed at me like twin suns. "I would never step on your hand!" he said. "Jesus, what gave you that idea?" He picked me up and carried me away.

Later—clean, but still agonized over the theft of my shoe—I felt anger. Something had been taken from me, easily; candy from a baby. The Back Bay was capricious and unaccountable.

"Where is my shoe?" I asked dad that night at dinner.

"Gone," he said. "The bog got it."

"What's a bog?" I asked.

"It's a place like the Back Bay," he answered.

There were no bogs in Southern California. It would have been more accurate for him to simply call it the "Back Bay." Or he might have taken a pedagogical approach by introducing me to the term "coastal estuary." But, characteristically, he chose the imagination of romanticism over the precision of technical terms.

Sometimes, even a single word can open a window on the submerged past. While I was sniffing the air and picking up shells, my father's inherited mind and vision was engaged in a survey of the estuary, taking an unconscious inventory—mud, water, the stench of decay, the silent vigor of birds as they fed, the treacherous ground underfoot that had tried to snatch his child away—and matching the seen and unseen with something he'd heard about, but had never seen. He used the word "bog" ritualistically, knowing, at a level below conscious recall, that—but for great-great-grandfather's emigration—he would have yanked me out of the Irish mud in Armagh, where sphagnum bogs do, in fact, exist. In a place where there were no bogs, the word made one and forged reciprocity between the immigrant and the assimilated.

"Quagmire, swampland, morass: the slime kingdoms"— the words of Seamus Heaney, in a poem titled "Kinship," describe a layered landscape sunk under the acidic waters of a bog. The bog preserved artifacts from ancient Ireland: a skeleton of a huge elk and the remnants of fir trees, submerged thousands of years ago when Ireland's climax forests held great tracts of deciduous and coniferous trees that grew and grew and grew.

Our estuary was a time capsule, too, and it held ages in its grasp. The bog had got my shoe and would preserve it.

The canvas would rot, but the rubber sole might not. Someone, thousands of years in the future, might lift the shoe from the depths of the slime and note its size and question my fate. Did the child survive?

Another landscape with my dad, almost forty years later. After he died of a heart attack (congestive heart failure is a direct genetic inheritance for all Creely men), I decided to scatter his ashes. I was living in San Francisco's Mission District—a stone's throw from my great-great-grandfather's house.

In the credulous culture of the New Age, as I've experienced it in Northern California, Irish and Celtic histories tend to get confused with each other, which has created some enduring myths about the Irish and what they worshipped and how. This cultural mash-up has always annoyed me—do people really believe the Irish consulted a tree zodiac?—but the eclecticism of the New Age ritual community can be hard to resist: I was persuaded, in spite of my preference for historical specificity, to lay down my defenses and find an oak grove in which to scatter my father's ashes. My dad, a bookseller by trade and temperament, was a quiet man who liked to escape the urgency of the twentieth century by reading widely, including (and especially) early Irish and Continental Celtic history and myth. Commemorating him both as an Irish American and latter-day Celt made sense.

My best friend Elyse thought she might know a place; she had spent her childhood exploring the Oakland Hills. We entered a trailhead one June afternoon with the late afternoon sun setting behind our backs. After twenty minutes of walking in Tilden Park, she directed my attention to the faint outline of a deer track, which ran up the side of a hill. We followed it into a small grove. A granite boulder sat in the dead center of a clearing. Over the boulder leaned an old Coast Live Oak. A group of graceful Bay Laurel trees lined the rear of the clearing. I inexpertly recited the chant of Aimhirghin, the oldest known Irish poem, for my father, a man who loved the great green world, and who was now in it and of it, peacefully.

For thousands of years, the stretch of coastal woodland in I which stood reciting Aimhirgin's words of perpetual becoming had been thick with native trees like Valley Oak, Redwood, and Bay Laurels. Under the pressure of urban development and natural disasters like the 1906 earthquake and fire, coastal woodlands were felled and used to build and rebuild San Francisco and other cities. A famous bar in San Francisco called the Redwood Room is an arboreal time capsule: the walls are paneled with old growth Redwood. California's trees tend to be entombed in buildings instead of bogs.

What remains of California's climax forests is a landscape punctuated by solitary trees. The iconic California oak tree—the city symbol of Oakland and subject of so many artistic renderings of the Golden State—sitting alone on top of a hill is a mark of tragedy. There should be many oaks instead of the lonely survivors so lovely, so desolate in their majestic singularity.

———

Singularity may yet be the fate of the California oak. In 1995, scientists at the University of Santa Cruz observed that large numbers of California oak trees were dying, quite suddenly. Closer investigation revealed the agent to be an unknown type of *Phytophthora*. Finding out that a *Phytophthora* pathogen was running amuck in California's coastal ecosystem didn't, as far as I know, cause a ripple of unease to spread throughout the Irish-American community of Northern California. But it frightened me. When I read the word *Phytophthora* in the paper, I shuddered, having made an inherited gesture of comparison.

I knew what the implications of an active *Phytophthora* blight were. I had taken classes in Irish history. I recalled my teacher, the late Daniel Cassidy, using clinically accurate terms in the classroom when speaking of the blight that ruined the potato crop. "*Phytophthora infestans,*" he would intone in his New York honk, "was the name of the fungus, which *only* destroyed potatoes. The famine was man-made." The wild microbial world in which the Creelys—in our latter-day incarnation as Californians—had spent heedless hours walking and hiking in, had in the past been turned against us. *Phytophthora*'s fungal power was unstoppable, unappeasable: it played by its own rules. *Phytophthora* could exert its power to radically reshape cultures, communities, history itself. It had done so before, to my family and to millions of others.

I scoured the local papers for any news of the oak tree blight. I felt no surprise, only resignation (and real fear) when I read that scientists at Berkeley thought that the oak killer might actually be *Phytophthora Infestans*, the ancient nemesis of the Irish. Was the killer mold that had destroyed the potato crops now bent on destroying California's oak trees? Was it stalking my family, taunting us with its invincibility? The oak tree has been a keystone species in every landscape my family has ever inhabited. The first occurrence of the patronymic "Creely" is found in County Derry, *Chontae Doire*, which is named after the great oak groves of Ireland. It all fit together.

It is now known that the oak killer is a cousin to the potato killer, a newer strain called *Phytophthora ramorum*. It is on the loose in California's coastal woodlands because of the preference of the commercial plant industry for non-native species. It is rapidly killing the California oak. As of this writing, there is no known cure and no solution.

In the late eighteenth century, an anonymous Gaelic poet looked at the denuded woodlands near Slieve na mBan, in Tipperary, and asked, plaintively, *Now what will we do for timber / with the last of the woods laid low?*

The oak tree that bends over the granite rock in the center of my dad's grove is still there. But for how long?

The interconnected nature of the forest is a tool, expertly wielded by the pathogen, which depends on the trees' proximity to one another. A raindrop crashing down on the leaf of a laurel tree will run down the trunk and into the soil. The pathogen swims in the tiny waterways of the sodden soil, making its way to a nearby oak. A cankerous spot appears on the trunk and the tree weeps precious sap. The oak tree dies within one to two months. No respite, no bargaining: just quiet death by water mold: sudden, silent and remorseless. And then a great transformation will change California. Instead of an oak tree bending over a stony boulder, there will be some poor substitute and only incoherent recollections of what used to grow there.

If the oak trees die, will anyone know why? Or will we instead put that story down and consign the trees we knew and loved to the inflexible and terrible category of the past?

In the future, when I tell stories of the California that I lived in, and that I sometimes call, privately and inaccurately, Daire Nua, the New Oak Grove, will anyone think to ask me this question: Why didn't the trees survive?

Maureen O'Connor

∾

Fearful Symmetry:
An Emigrant's Return
to Celtic Tiger Ireland

Every summer of the first twenty years of my life, I relived my parents' youngest days. I drank water from the same wells, carried on my clothes and hair the smoke of turf cut from the same bogs, feared the same ghosts and fairies in the long half-light of July nights. Those scenes have since changed, though they have long been resistant to the forward press of time and have not yet completely disappeared. I type this in an office overlooking the silver River Corrib in Galway, where swans drift and along which runs a busy motorway. Our annual returns to Ireland are over; we live here now, characters in what Helena Mulkerns has suggested "might be the next great Irish story," a story my father never imagined would be told.

———

Wet currant bush and clover are the smells that return my father to his childhood, a field sown with rock and briar and stinging nettle; damp, rushy, cold. The stark rasp of a rook, then silence. His sister Margaret coughed for days and nights with a sound he didn't recognize, and then she was silent. When he spent a year in bed with scarlet, and then rheumatic, fever, it was believed that what he had was polio, the crippler of children across the country at that time. A man with "the cure" was brought in, and the cure, when it came, was a miraculous one. His heart has murmured ever after.

My mother remembers him when he returned to school after that illness, his face white and wide as a waiting page. He shuffled slowly, watching the other boys at football. Before falling ill, he had dreamed of playing for the county. My parents attended the same school, Ballinameen National School, in north County Roscommon, a year apart. They said the same prayer every Sunday night: that the master would be dead before morning. The master, my father's uncle, did die fairly prematurely, in his late fifties—extinguished, no doubt, by the accumulated pressure of hundreds of desperately murmured pleas, though too late to afford my parents any relief. My father still says he hopes his uncle is suffering all the torments of hell. My mother remembers looking at the back of my father's head as they walked down the same road to school, past the church and churchyard, the old forge and the old chapel, and knowing that she would marry him. She has more stories about those days than my father does. My father's Ireland resembles Edna O'Brien's, "fervid, enclosed and catastrophic," while my mother's memories have more warmth and light and detail, down to the ditties rehearsed to remember spelling words. One of the words rendered into rhythm was Mississippi: "Mrs d Mrs i Mrs ffi Mrs c Mrs u Mrs lty"; a peculiar word for a child in the middle of rural Ireland to be memorizing. She seems to have had no premonitions about one day living within one-hundred-and-fifty miles of the river by that name.

My father's father had also been in the region of the Mississippi, decades earlier. He had worked in Illinois on the railroad in the late 1920s, with no intention of ever returning to Ireland until one of the three emigrant brothers, Matt, fell seriously ill and my grandfather, Brian (also called Bernard), drew the short straw when the decision was made to bring Matt home. Matt was awkward enough to recover and live on for several decades after returning to Ireland. Jim, the brother who remained in the United States, settled in Brooklyn, married, and opened a grocery store. The family dispersal to America resumed when my father, the eldest of five surviving children, was eventually sent to his Uncle Jim, as were two brothers after him. Just a few weeks after turning fifteen, he sailed for America. A neighbor drove my father and his father down to Cork, a long day's journey at the time. In Cobh, my father stood in his best clothes looking down at the shallow water of the bay—his first sight of the ocean—and asked his father how could that be the sea when it wasn't blue. The hotel where they stayed the night of their arrival was still overlooking Cobh harbor five years ago when my father told me this story, standing in the same spot, looking at the same oily, gray-green sea.

In May of 1950, just as emigration from Ireland was about to reach its highest levels since the nineteenth century, Seán Connor—who in America would become Jack O'Connor—sailed on the *New Amsterdam* for New York. On the trip over he won one-hundred-and-fifty dollars on a greyhound racing game. He did not at that time, or indeed for many years, regard this piece of luck as an emblem. In Brooklyn, he lived with his Uncle Jim, Jim's wife, Eileen, and with their two children, Margaret and Johnnie. My father attended Fort Hamilton High School, where he endured some teasing about his accent and his clothes. But he was mostly ignored. Because he was tall and good looking, fairly good at basketball, and quietly friendly, his country awkwardness and oddly formal way of dressing were subject to only mild, bored abuse by the slick teenagers in leather jackets whose interest in cars absorbed their energies.

By his senior year he had acquired a greasy ducktail and a leather jacket of his own as well as something of a smirk. His Latin teacher encouraged him to lose his Irish accent, a kind intention that my father considered humiliating interference. She is the only high school teacher he now remembers. He was expected to work every spare hour in his uncle's store, a durance under which he chafed. His last job in Ireland had been working for a grocer in Boyle, a cruel man who had boys do jobs too hard and heavy for them to add a righteous savor to his abuse. Life in New York seemed as miserable, narrow, and stony in its own way as what my father had left behind. All that made him feel less lonesome was the arrival, in time, of his younger brothers.

After high school, unsure what he wanted to do beyond somehow getting far away from Bay Ridge, Brooklyn, he took college courses in accounting, and then joined the army. When he joined in 1955, the war was over, but American troops still occupied Korea. Basic training was in Fort Dix, New Jersey. Six months later, the thousand or so recruits with whom he had trained were divided up and shipped to various camps around the country. My father was in the group that headed down to El Paso, Texas for anti-aircraft-gun training. The two weeks of slow bus travel through the segregated South shocked him, as he had so far seen little of America beyond the clamorous heterogeneity of the boroughs of New York. He had already been disquieted by his encounters with Irish-American clannish-ness, xenophobia, and outright racism, but he had never seen the victims of discrimination so conquered, so sub-missive. To this day he has never been able to describe what he saw there, reluctant to add in any way to the degradation and humiliation he was himself ashamed to witness. His sorrowful discovery of the legislated discrimi-nation of the Jim Crow laws recalled to him Ireland's Penal Laws and centuries of racially justified brutality suf-fered by the "native" Irish.

Struggling, as he did, with his belief that he had been rejected and ejected without recourse, my father did not especially long for Ireland, even in his loneliest times away from it. Nonetheless, he felt inexorably claimed by it, linked to it by what Edna O'Brien has described as the "tie that is more umbilical than among any other race on earth." He was, and continues to be, moved by Ireland's history of violent oppressions and dispossessions. His father had tried to resurrect the "O" in O'Connor, erased over the generations by the imperatives of Anglicizisation. While in my grandfather's time, the family remained "Connor" to those who knew them despite his efforts, my father, his brothers, and his sister all honored their father's desire for reclamation. Now, except to a few surviving bachelor farm-ers around Ballinameen, we are once more O'Connors. This same grandfather fought for the nation's indepen-dence, had even been imprisoned by the crown and dra-matically dynamited out of jail. My grandfather and his brother Jim had been especially alarmed by Matt's illness in America because Matt had been "delicate" since the day and night he spent hiding from the Black and Tans, sub-merged in a bog hole, breathing through a reed. Bred on tales and taught to sing songs of resisting the powerful and their injustices, my father had expected to find sympathy and solidarity among the disinherited of the world.

He was shipped to Korea and to stultifying boredom, a condition he considered worse than all the physical discomforts he suffered there. He had enjoyed the clean baking heat and sere beauty of the Texas desert, the trips across the Rio Grande to Mexico where the people reminded him of the Irish by bearing their poverty with a similar kind of sardonic cheerfulness, exhibiting a familiarly ambivalent warmth, expansive and yet wary, provisional. In Korea, he enountered a different heat and new kind of penetrating damp: swampy and nauseating. He learned just how various and intense bad smells could be, including those contributed by the decomposing bodies of Koreans that hung from the gates of the Turkish compound, whose food supplies the starving men had attempted to break into.

When his tour of duty ended, my father made his first trip back to Ireland: he was the glamorous and interesting GI returning to his homeplace that Frank McCourt hoped to be in his memoir '*Tis*. While McCourt's fantasy of being considered "gorgeous," whispered about and admired by the girls of Limerick, ended when he was recognized as "just someone from the back lanes of Limerick all togged out in the American uniform," my father's GI uniform did get him the girl. He visited local families, including the Flanagans down the road. Mrs. Flanagan wondered aloud how it was that the United States Army had not been able to get Seán Connor to stop slouching, then sent her daughter, Colette, out to say hello to the returned Yank, who was talking to her father and brothers out footing the turf. Though unwilling to please either her mother or the visitor whom she saw as a self-satisfied Yank, and determined not to be charmed, Colette nonetheless greeted the visitor and relented so far as to attend a dance with him that night. For the next several weeks, they conducted their courtship in Athlone, where my mother worked in the Palace Bar, and before my father returned to the States, they were engaged.

Six months later, my mother left everything she knew and joined my father in Brooklyn, where they married in St. Anselm's church in January of 1958. New York was terse and dirty, noisy and blurred with noise and motion. The exotically pungent pressed everywhere, speaking rapidly in languages that might have included English. My mother found unendurable what she interpreted as the brusque anger she encountered in every shop, bank, post office, subway station. She could neither understand what anyone was saying nor make herself understood. She worked briefly as a switchboard operator and for a time managed to channel her soft midlands drawl into straighter, crisper lines, but resigned in embarrassment the day she was laughed at for her "rustic" misunderstanding of what was meant when someone was referred to as being "out in the field." In the shifting, sharp-elbowed spaces wrested from the unrelenting crowds, she became so thin she had to buy her clothes in the children's department.

My father was by this time working for Aer Lingus, which transferred him to Chicago—a less harrying city than New York that my mother found almost pastoral in comparison. She dressed again as a grown-up, and her life settled into a pattern familiar to middle-class Americans. She and my father had two children, bought a house, got a dog, drove a station wagon, and my father opened a successful travel business, specializing in Irish tours and charters. He prospered. He was able to send his children to university, the immigrant's ambition fulfilled. He regards emigration as modern Ireland's greatest tragedy, yet he is grateful to the country that made his story a successful one. After Korea, he became a United States citizen, something my mother was slow to do, as she considered it somehow disloyal. I was in fourth grade before she took this step, and I remember quizzing her on American history in preparation for the citizenship exam. My father inculcated into my brother and me a fervid patriotism that was neither complacent nor uncritical of the great country it was our fortune to be born into—he has never stopped hurting from what he saw on the bus trip between New Jersey and El Paso—nor did it in any way weaken our attachment to the place where he and my mother were born. When as a small girl standing at my school desk I swallowed tears while singing "My Country 'Tis of Thee," the land where my fathers died was at once Ireland and America.

Being a travel agent meant my father could bring us all to Ireland regularly. I made my first trip "home," as I have always heard it called, at the age of six months, and my family spent every subsequent summer in Ireland. We stayed in the same house my father had been born in. My brother and I walked the same fields and boreens, jumped the same ditches, and swung on the same gates that my parents had known. It was just as cold and damp as it had ever been, with streaming walls and blistered wallpaper and chill morning linoleum and hot water bottles in bed in the middle of July. But I loved the rubber bottle in its little knitted jacket, which I treated as a baby doll, and the cross-beamed ceiling that reminded me every morning where I was just before I became aware of the slowly building bubble of a hen's cluck bursting at the bedroom window. I loved the smoky smell of the kitchens, going to the well with my grandmothers, feeding the hens and gathering their eggs, the home-made pillows from which we plucked different colored feathers, tea towels drying on the hedge, even the vividly dead spider behind the glass of a picture frame, poised everlastingly just above the eye of some ancestor-priest that hung over my bed. I imagined the priest had been bleached to that faint brown-gold tracery by his plump fellow inmate. The faded priest frowned imploringly at the Sacred Heart hanging opposite. Jesus always seemed to be gazing back sympathetically, his head to one side, "a bit like a kitten," in the memorable simile of Roddy Doyle's *Paddy Clarke.*

The rest of the dreary year, when we were back in school in America, walking through the snow, forgetting our overshoes, losing our mittens, my brother and I dreamed, awake and sleeping, of a sky that touched the ground, as if, when tumbling down the hill, you could fall right in, of that sky's active miscellany of clouds, their bronze bellies and purple depths casting shapes of darker purple on the rain-brightened hills. We longed to ride again atop the quaking hay being brought in from the fields, drawn by blinkered horses whose massive sides shivered at the lightest touch. We delighted in the flower-pocked grass that reached over the top of our wellies, the meadowsweet and buttercups and thistles breaking on all our senses, the sweet stacked hay; sorrel, and rust-spotted dock leaves, even the cow pats and what to call them in Irish. We even enjoyed the agonizing shiver inspired by the dark frowsty outdoor toilet, belled with moss and lichen, two worn steps down to where spiders and daddy long-legs lay in wait for a bared bottom and where the sound of cattle rubbing and breathing was spookily near, seeming to mist the cold, close air. My brother and I agreed that there were only two objectionable things about these summers: one was being put to bed in broad daylight; the other was the thick, warm milk, which in my uncle's house was sometimes fly-specked. But there were cows and bulls, horses, donkeys, hens, sheep, baby animals of all kinds when we would arrive in early June, and best of all, dogs simply every-where. My uncle's dog Towser ran after me all summer long staging one unnecessary rescue after another, like a canine television star. The day we were leaving, and only on that day, when driving back to Shannon, another of my uncle's dogs, Prince, would chase the car for miles down the narrow rutted road out. He ran so far and for so long, we felt one of our hearts must burst.

In 1997, more than forty-five years after my father left the country, my brother Seán and his wife Denise relocated to Ireland, eventually settling in the house where my father was born on top of Sheerevagh Hill, named for the fairy mound there. He has two Irish-born daughters who are growing up in the dream landscape of our childhood summers. It is the background of their everyday lives. Of course, there have been changes, including the fact that most of the farm has been turned over to forestry.

But there are continuities as well, uncanny elisions and symmetries the likes of which my parents could not have envisioned in Bay Ridge in 1958. My brother's eldest, another Colette, started attending Ballinameen National School in September, 2004, the school where her grandparents first met. My parents have retired and also moved to Ireland in 2001. I relocated here in 2003. My parents live on the shores of Lough Key not far from their homeplace. My father often collects his granddaughter from school, retracing a journey he thought long concluded, what Edna O'Brien calls "that trenchant childhood route." He passes the chapel at the bottom of Sheerevagh Hill and the churchyard where his parents and little sister Margaret are buried. Ballinameen, once a mere crossroads village that appeared only on the most detailed of maps, is now becoming a town. There are fifty new houses between the pub and the graveyard and more under construction. Parasolled tables appear in the summer sun outside that pub, no longer the dark and quiet, low-ceilinged, men's-only retreat it had been for generations. The smoking ban has meant not only a cleaner, brighter interior, but also more movement and noise, as smokers regularly step outside and make the place seem less enclosed. Rooks still cry overhead, nesting as they've always done in the massive yew trees, but now mobile phones also trill and beep and the pub's television plays music videos, featuring a new kind of dancing at this particular crossroads.

My father had been mostly pleased with the changes the Celtic Tiger has brought to Ireland, the prosperity and cheer, and above all the astonishing decrease in emigration, but the new materialism and preoccupation with status dismays him. The profit to be gained from internationalism has rendered the national irrelevant and outdated. After fifty years in America, he does not feel at home in Ireland, yet he objects to the Americanization of its culture, to the loss of regionalism, including accents, to the depressing blandness of tastes determined by television.

Exile creates such unsettled and unsettling ironies of allegiance. Of her own emigration, Edna O'Brien said that "leaving is only conditional." My father has now left two places, two homes from which he has grown to feel ever more alienated, the condition of return to or retrieval of the homeland less realizable. Every homeland he has known has become a strange country, his own history less narratable even as the circle appears to neatly close. The present threatens to debase the coin of his past. When he saw the images from Abu Ghraib last year, his distress was profound. He felt ashamed of America for the first time, personally affronted, as if his own wearing of the country's uniform had been betrayed, defiled. Then, later in the year, the passage of the citizenship referendum in Ireland–which means that a child born on Irish soil is now no longer automatically entitled to citizenship–revealed a prosperous country unwelcoming of immigrants, such as he was himself fifty years ago when he arrived in another prosperous, industrial land.

His restlessness is inconsolable lately. My mother recently asked to see a smile in the morning. He went out, built a little cairn of stones outside the window, and painted a yellow smiley face on it. He spends a great deal of time outside on his own, digging holes, piling stones, clipping hedges, walking and walking. The idealism bred into him as a boy in Ireland and that flourished in his years in America grows ever more remote, fabular. In June of 2004, even as the citizenship referendum was being debated, the Bloomsday centenary dominated the Irish news. My father, who reads everything, was struck by something in one of the thumbnail Joyce biographies larding every paper in the run-up to June 16. The piece described Joyce as having "a homeless mind."

He spread the article in front of me and tapped the page. "That's me," he said, "I am a homeless mind."

~

CONTRIBUTORS

James Silas Rogers edits *New Hibernia Review*, a journal of Irish Studies published by the University of St. Thomas in Minnesota. He served as president of the American Conference for Irish Studies (ACIS) from 2009-2011. He frequently presents on Irish-American writing at ACIS and other conferences and has published articles on Irish-American literature in such journals as *Studies, Études Irlandaises, the Canadian Journal of Irish Studies,* and *US Catholic Historian.* With Matthew O'Brien, he co-edited *After the Flood: Irish America 1945-1960* (Irish Academic Press, 2009).

Daniel Tobin is the author of six books of poems, *Where the World Is Made* (1999); *Double Life* (2005); *The Narrows* (2005), in which the work presented here is the title poem; *Second Things* (2008); *Belated Heavens* (2010), the winner of the Massachusetts Book Award in Poetry; and *The Net* (forthcoming from Four Way Books, 2014), along with the critical studies *Passage to the Center* and *Awake in America: On Irish American Poetry.* He is the editor of *The Book of Irish American Poetry from the Eighteenth Century to the Present; Light in Hand: The*

Selected Poems of Lola Ridge; and *Poet's Work, Poet's Play.* His awards include fellowships from the National Endowment for the Arts and the John Simon Guggenheim Foundation. His website is http://www.danieltobin.org/.

James Murphy was born to immigrant parents and raised in Brooklyn, New York. He was the first in his family to attend college, earning a B. A, from Manhattan College, an M.A. from Niagara University, and a Ph.D. from Temple University. He began the Irish Studies Program at Villanova University in 1979. Now retired, he and his wife Kath divide their time between Pennsylvania and their home in Galway City. He is working on a book-length memoir.

Christine Cusick is Associate Professor of English and Director of the Honors Program at Seton Hill University. Her research focuses on the intersections of ecology and cultural memory. She has published ecocritical readings of contemporary Irish poetry, fiction, bogland photography, and American nature writing. Her edited collection *Out of the Earth: Ecocritical Readings of Irish Texts* was published by Cork University Press in 2010. Her most recent essay appears in *The Bioregional Imagination: New Perspectives on Literature, Ecology and Place* (2012). She is currently co-editing a collection to be titled *Unfolding Irish Landscapes: The Spatial Identities of Tim Robinson* (2012) and is working on a collection of nonfiction essays. Her essay here was chosen as one of the year's "notable essays" in *Best American Essays* (2008). She lives with her family at the foothills of the Laurel Mountains in western Pennsylvania.

Brian Nerney is Chair and Associate Professor in the Communication, Writing and the Arts Department at Metropolitan State University, a leading institution for adult learners, in St. Paul, Minnesota. An active member of the American Conference for Irish Studies, he writes about Irish-American families and how they are shaped by the stories they tell or deliberately withhold. He is also working on a study of John McCarten, an Irish-American who wrote for *The New Yorker* magazine for many years. He has written previously about the magazine, including the first evaluation of Katharine S. White's influence on *The New Yorker's* early years. Nerney lives with his family in St. Paul. His essay here was chosen as one of the year's "notable essays" in *Best American Essays* (2010).

James Doan holds a B.A. in Literature from U.C., Santa Cruz, an M.A. in Folklore and Mythology from U.C.L.A., an M.A. in Celtic Languages and Literatures, as well as a Ph.D. in Folklore and Celtic Studies from Harvard. Originally from Palo Alto, California, he is a professor of humanities at Nova Southeastern University (NSU) in Ft. Lauderdale, where he teaches courses in literature and the arts, and folklore and mythology. He has published extensively in the areas of Irish and Celtic studies and is currently working on a play titled *The Irish Dracula: A Melodrama in Five Acts.*

Brigittine M. French is an Associate Professor of Anthropology at Grinnell College in Iowa. Her research centers on relationships among collective identity formation, discourse, and culture in charged political contexts. She is the author of *Maya Ethnolinguistic Identity: Violence, Cultural Rights and Modernity in Highland Guatemala* (2010, University of Arizona Press) along with numerous articles that include: "Ethnography and 'Post-Conflict' Violence in the Irish Free State" in the *American Anthropologist* and "Linguistic Science and Nationalist Revolution: Expert Knowledge and the Making of Sameness in Pre-Independence Ireland" in *Language in Society*. She is currently working on a project that deals with courtroom language, gender, and citizenship in Irish district courts.

Lawrence J. McCaffrey is Professor Emeritus of History at Loyola University of Chicago. In 1954, he received his Ph.D. from the University of Iowa. McCaffrey has written and edited a number of books on Irish and Irish-American history, published articles on the same subjects and Irish and Irish-American literature. In 1960, he co-founded the American Conference for Irish Studies. McCaffrey has served as president of ACIS and of the American Catholic Historical Association. He was a consultant to and appeared in the 1997 documentary *The Irish in America: Long Journey Home* and technical advisor to the 2002 film *The Road to Perdition*. In 1982, St Ambrose University, his undergraduate alma mater, awarded McCaffrey with an Honorary Doctor of Humanities; five years later the National University of Ireland designated him Honorary Doctor of Letters.

Aífe Murray lives and works in San Francisco. A transdisciplinary writer interested in stories that have been erased or covered over, her latest project is about her grandmother's incendiary encounters with the Ku Klux Klan. She collaborated with Emily Dickinson Museum house cleaners and gardeners on the artists' book *Art of Service*. She has created and led tours of Amherst, Massachusetts, from the perspective of Emily Dickinson's servants for the Mead Art Museum exhibition *Word as Object: Emily Dickinson and Contemporary Art* and for the Emily Dickinson Museum. "A Yankee Poet's Irish Headwaters" appeared in a slightly different form in her book *Maid as Muse: How Servants Changed Emily Dickinson's Life and Language* (UPNE/UNH 2010), which was a finalist for the Northern California Book Award. Her web site is http://maidasmuse.com/

James Liddy was born in Dublin in 1934 and educated at University College Dublin and the King's Inns. The founding editor of *Arena* magazine, Liddy was already a prominent literary figure in Ireland when he emigrated to the United States in 1967. He joined the English faculty at the University of Wisconsin-Milwaukee in 1976, and taught there until his death in 2008. The author of numerous collections of poetry, Liddy was a member of Aosdána, the Irish Academy of Arts and Letters. The essay presented here appeared in a slightly different form in the first of his two volumes of memoir, *The Doctor's House: An Autobiography* (2004).

Thomas B. O'Grady was born and grew up on Prince Edward Island. He has been Director of Irish Studies at the University of Massachusetts Boston since 1984. He is also currently Director of the Creative Writing Program there. He writes frequently on Irish literary and cultural matters. His reviews and essays on Irish literary and cultural matters have been published in a wide variety of scholarly journals on both sides of the Atlantic, including *Éire-Ireland, James Joyce Quarterly, Études Irlandaises, and Irish University Review.* His poems and short stories have been widely published. His first book of poems, *What Really Matters,* was published by McGill-Queen's University Press in 2000. He has completed the manuscript for a second volume of poems, and is completing a manuscript for a volume of short fiction.

Charles Fanning is a retired teacher and scholar of Irish-American studies. He is the author of numerous books and articles, the most well-known of which is *The Irish Voice in America: 250 Years of Irish-American Fiction* (1990). He is still writing essays, most recently about pianist Eleanor Kane Neary, the comics master George McManus, and Irish-American culture in the 1930s. A native New Englander, he now lives in Carbondale, Illinois, having retired from the state university there in 2007. "Lodestone: Following the Emly Shrine" appeared in somewhat different form in *Mapping Norwood: An Irish-American Memoir* (University of Massachusetts Press, 2010).

Eamonn Wall, a native of Co. Wexford, emigrated to the USA in 1982. He is a graduate of University College, Dublin, the University of Wisconsin-Milwaukee, and the CUNY Graduate Center where he received his Ph.D. in English. He is the author of six collections of poetry, most recently *Sailing Lake Mareotis* (2011) and two prose works, *Writing the Irish West: Ecologies and Traditions* (University of Notre Dame Press, 2011) and *From the Sin-é Cafe to the Black Hills: Notes on the New Irish* (University of Wisconsin Press, 2000). "The Black Hills, The Gorey Road" appeared in a slightly different form in that volume. Wall is a Professor of English and Smurfit Chair of Irish Studies at the University of Missouri-St. Louis. His essay here was chosen as one of the year's "notable essays" in *Best American Essays* (1999).

Elizabeth Creely is a fourth-generation Californian who received an M.F.A. from San Francisco State University. In addition to her work in *New Hibernia Review,* she has published personal essays in the *Mississippi Review, Dogwood Journal,* and in the forthcoming anthology *Manifest West: Eccentricities of Geography* by Western Press Books. A devoted cyclist, Creely writes a column on cycling in San Francisco and the Bay Area for SF Examiner.com. She is currently researching Patricia Maginnis, a 1960s-era reproductive rights activist. Her essay here was listed as one of the year's "notable essays" in *Best American Essays* (2012).

Maureen O'Connor is a lecturer in English at University College Cork, Ireland. She has published widely on Irish writers including Lady Morgan, Maria Edgeworth, Charles Maturin, Oscar Wilde, Somerville and Ross, Frances Power Cobbe, James Joyce, Mary O'Malley, Éilis Ní Dhuibhne, and Edna O'Brien. She is the editor of *Back to the Future: Festschrift for Tadhg Foley* (Peter Lang, 2010), and co-editor of *India and Ireland: Colonies, Culture, and Empire* (with Tadhg Foley; Irish Academic Press, 2006); *Edna O'Brien: New Critical Perspectives* (with Kathryn Laing and Sinéad Mooney; Carysfort, 2006); *Wild Colonial Girl: Essays on Edna O'Brien* (with Lisa Colletta; Wisconsin, 2006). She is the author of *The Female and the Species: The Animal in Irish Women's Writing* (Peter Lang, 2009) as well as a forthcoming book on Edna O'Brien. Her current research is on nation and nature in the work of the early Irish feminist writers and activists Eva Gore-Booth, Margaret Cousins, and Charlotte Despard. Born in Chicago, she currently divides her time between Galway and Cork.